Journeyman

Diana, Heysel, the Hand of God and Me

Paul Fry

Proactive Media

For Pam

Contents

Title Page   1

Copyright   2

Dedication   3

Foreword   7

1 Thanks for the memories   10

2 Early doors   17

3 To be sure   30

4 School days   40

5 Nobel   45

6 New Town   58

7 Read All About It   69

8 Earning my stripes   84

9 Lords of the Rings   98

10 Rocky roads   111

11 Graham Poll only booked me once   117

12 Glenda   129

13 Street of Shame   136

14 This Sporting Life   148

15 Everyone Out   164

16 Heysel   171

17 Tragedy and mystery   183

18 Messiah and Naughty Boy   195

19 He Wears It Well   206

20 Hand of God   219

21 All Systems Go   229

22 People's Princess   242

23 Hold the Entire Paper   256

24 King Kenny's Bouncy Balls   266

25 Kia Ora in Kiwiland   278

26 Looking Back. And Ahead   299

About The Author   311

Foreword

By John Sellers, of Firststone Publishing

I remember meeting Paul Fry for the first time when he was introduced to the rest of the staff in the North Herts Gazette newsroom. The new kid on the block had a ready smile and an easy charm... and looked all of 15 years old.

But if we were disinclined to take our new cub reporter seriously, it was at our peril. A few months later he snatched a major scoop involving Spurs legends Gilzean and Greaves from under my nose and I realised we had a serious journalist on our hands.

As the crow flies it is less than 30 miles from Stevenage to Fleet Street, but it can be a long and tortuous journey. Plenty catch the bus; not so many make it to the final stop.

The pair of us pitched up at Mirror Group a few years apart, and were both working there when Robert Maxwell was laying waste to both working conditions and editorial standards.

I cried enough and left for the world of publishing, but Paul had printer's ink in his veins. He headed next for the Mail On Sunday and, more than 40 years after he began, the rookie reporter is still, first and always, a newspaperman.

His career, and an insatiable love of sport, has brought him alongside the great and the good... and sometimes too close to the news for comfort. He was within touching distance of the tragedy at Heysel Stadium, in which 39 football fans lost their lives and 600 more were hurt. The likes of Diego Maradona and Princess Diana are part of Paul's story. But the most compelling part of all is his journey into the past to discover the family he never knew.

We have stayed in touch ever since his first day, bound by a shared passion for Stevenage football club, and worked together on various books in the intervening years, usually with football as the theme. There is one such project that epitomises the complete professional.

We were commissioned to produce a big colour number ahead of the 2000 European Championships...the kind of book you see piled high and sold cheap in Motorway services.

Stars Of Euro 2000 was to be a series of in-depth

interviews with the leading players who would appear in the finals. But waiting until the finalists were resolved meant we were left with a very short editorial timeframe.

Several weeks setting up interviews and criss-crossing Europe by plane might have done the trick. Paul had a fortnight, and a travel budget that stretched as far as the Tube fare to the Mirror cuttings library, to write the whole thing.

Two weeks on, the 'whole thing' arrived on my desk. Word perfect...and indistinguishable from a series of audiences with soccer's elite. Above all, one 'interview' sticks in my memory... with Turkey's golden boy Hakan Sukur, who scored goals for fun and was the main reason Turkey made the last 16.

It contained the immortal line: "As we drank coffee together on the terrace of a cafe overlooking the Bosphorus, Hakan leaned forward and told me..." Simply priceless. I swear you can smell the Sobranie smoke.

A life in print journalism can be a heady mixture of inspiration and perspiration, of meeting impossible deadlines when you are running on empty.

If you want to know what it is really like, warts and all, this is the book for you. Read all about it...

1 Thanks for the memories

The thing about writing the story of your own life is that if you can't recall exactly what happened, you can simply make it up. Not that this is intended to be a work of 'faction'. But while I have recourse to at least some fragments of memory, it is subjective and sometimes does not bear scrutiny.

That said, I have done my best to tally my account with names and dates where possible and try to give as honest an account as I can. I have skipped some parts – often the more painful memories, as I think they are best left where they belong – even though others might find it cathartic to address their sad moments.

It is nevertheless true that we tend to remember the most life-changing and dramatic experiences the best and clearest. And as I have found from this exercise, jotting stuff down mostly for the benefit of my family and friends, memory is curious in that it can be triggered by any of our five senses; that smell of rhubarb and custard that your mother used to cook, the fat rhubarb freshly picked from the patch at the top of the garden, behind the swings but which you can't recall having since childhood.

Or it could be a once-familiar record that takes you back to the common room you used at school. With me that was Freda Payne's Band of Gold, a proper Holland-Dozier-Holland ear-worm from 1970 that was No.1 for six weeks. Or a detour to a haunt from your youth; the park that was your Wembley Stadium, your Lord's cricket ground - the place you also had that first illicit cigarette or a first, embarrassed and awkward teenage kiss.

Kernels of memory are not stored away neatly, in chronological order from left to right like an obsessive's album collection, so that you can dust them off and revisit them, while remembering to replace them in the right place to be found at a later date.

No, they are more like a typical teenager's bedroom – fragments are not so much discarded as strewn everywhere. Oddly, teens have this capacity to delve beneath the empty yoghurt pots, crisp packets and piles of dirty laundry and still find the thing they are looking for – unless, of course, it was the homework they had forgotten to do, the dog had eaten and they are now desperate to get sorted on the bus to school.

Computer nerds call that RAM (which stands for Random Access Memory). Parts of data are stored in a haphazard way, not sequentially. The system keeps a central 'roadmap' of where all the pieces are located and can reassemble them faster than a Government minister can spin a lie. Human memories are a lot like that, only our central roadmap is less reliable. It can be prone to illness, injury or trauma.

Nowadays I find myself drifting into a kind of stereotypical old person state, where I can't recall what I was doing yesterday or the week before, and yet other times are much more cogent. I do the typical thing of going upstairs for something, only to forget what it was, and have to retrace my steps. Going to the shops for three things is a recipe for coming back with the least important two.

One particularly enlightening demonstration into the effects of stress on memory happened after I suffered a bereavement. I had driven to Peterborough to have a lunch and go shopping with my daughter, Stefanie. When it came to the drive back home, I could not find my keys.

So, I retraced my steps back to the multi-storey to find my car on the top floor where I had left it, with the keys in the ignition and the engine running. I was horrified – how would I have explained that to the insurance company? Luckily, my fogged brain had cost me only a quarter of a tank of petrol.

So I don't trust my roadmap entirely. All too frequently I call into question the truth of what I recollect. As I say, I will endeavour to be truthful with the more salient stuff – but the fringy bits may be somewhat more flaky. It is for you to judge.

Perhaps you shared some of my journey with me, if only for a few stops, and recall things differently. That is understandable. If you have ever been to a boxing match, you will be only too aware how judges, sitting on different sides of the ring, can come to very opposite conclusions on the outcome of the fight. One judge might see a punch actually land. Another, from his vantage point, might think it missed completely. Or you might just be contrary. Perish the thought that I might be wrong; I am only human after all.

This story is very much about the life of a journeyman journalist. Others have had more distinguished careers, seen far more, done more. But my journey has been unique and thus, I feel, worthy of retelling.

I delve into my search for my birth family - something I felt I needed to do to better understand myself. And yet we all too often describe ourselves solely by the job we do or our role in life. I wish that were not the case. As a trainee reporter, you are taught to find a label for the person who is the subject of the story; something to personalise them. So it is a 47-year-old mum of two, or 26-year-old bus driver, not simply a local man or woman.

I have tried not to define myself in this way but if I get retire to collect the state pittance, er pension, I will have done 47 years in the same profession; pretty much a lifetime. Labels will undoubtedly be more fluid as time goes on. Even now, we live in an age of insecure, often zero-hours work where too many people do more than one job, out of necessity, and others are having to retrain mid-career because they have been made redundant when their trade or role is no more.

I have seen it in so many industries, mine among

them. Hundreds of papers have closed in the past 15 years and thousands of journos are now inhabiting other worlds, lost to the dissemination of trustworthy news.

In that sense, I am very much from a bygone age but hopefully not entirely a dinosaur in my own fast-changing industry. I will talk more of that elsewhere, as a passionate believer that communities need local news sources, and democracy is the poorer for their demise.

I have often thought 47 years was a long time to be in the same industry but recall how when I was a junior reporter, I interviewed people who had been with the same company for 50 years. I have scratched my head of late at how they could have done that and still retired at 65. But in 1944, the school-leaving age rose from 14 to 15. It had been 13 at one time. So these people were indeed able to have clocked up a half century of toil.

That milestone will soon be the norm again as the retirement age rises inexorably, possibly in the hope that many don't live long enough to receive their paltry state payout. That is, of course, an entirely political decision and glosses over the fact that while we will indeed have a burgeoning elderly population, we also have another baby boom, with a huge cohort youngsters now entering their teens. They will one day be paying taxes to support the older generation.

I digress. My experiences have of course fed into my opinions and political leanings. But they have been underpinned by my morals from an upbringing as an adopted infant, a council estate boy and youth shaped by a stable family in a shiny New Town.

It could have been very different for me, judging by the life my half-brother and sisters had – and these were people I never knew existed until I was in my fifties. I thus became ever more appreciative of being able to take a very different fork in the road on my journey through life.

I had the benefit of going to a good grammar school, for a couple of years, at least. It switched to comprehensive after my second year, though we stayed in the grammar stream. But some of the better teachers fled to schools they saw as being more worthy of their talents.

I could have had a free university education, something denied to today's generations, but turned it down. Having flunked my O-levels, I stayed back a year at school and then and went on to college with a firm plan to get into newspapers.

There has always been something of the voyeur about me, I think, as someone happy to observe and see the funny, quirky side of life. And I have seen, as you will discover from this book.

The bad news for you is that it has whetted my appetite to write more. You don't have to read it, of course. But you know you want to... just in case you get a little mention.

If just one person enjoys this, my hours of toil – even before the 2020 great spring lockdown when

I was furloughed for so long that I was able to make serious progress with this project and my colleagues dubbed me the 'Furlough King', will have been worthwhile. At least I had some fun going back through my archives.

One colleague – who had a huge influence on my formative career – told me when I was a wet-behind-the-ears trainee reporter, "You've got to do this job for a lot of years, so you might has well enjoy it. Do it for yourself, and hope others enjoy what you turn out.

"If nothing else, it beats the crap out of working for a living."

He was not wrong.

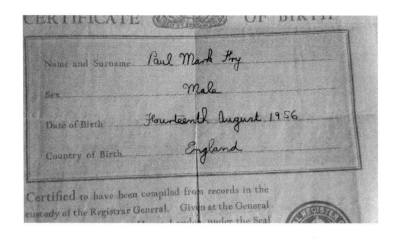

2 Early doors

I have tried hard not to start off with the words, 'I was born on...' But, in mitigation, there seems to have been such little thought about the issue of my conception, perhaps I am justified in not putting in too much effort myself.

So... I was born on August 14, 1956. If I now had only my original birth certificate, which is the size of a small pocket handkerchief, that would be all I could tell you. It is nonetheless a special piece of paper, reserved for children who have been adopted. I can add that it was issued on May 9,

1958, when my adoption was complete. There is no mention of either parent's name on what is such an important document – but there are the additional "nuggets" that I was male and born in England. It singled me out as being different. But although I was in care from birth and might indeed have been like the last turkey in the shop on Christmas Eve, I did soon find a loving home. So many children, sadly, do not and their life chances can be blighted forever.

Too many never know that feeling of being wanted or loved. While I was born in an era when abortion was illegal, such procedures were still undertaken in back streets, so I indeed count my blessings.

This is not a bleeding-heart account designed to win your sympathy. It is just that I have learned so much about myself by combing back through my past. And, as I get older, combing through my hair has become somewhat easier, too. And why doesn't the barber clip only the grey ones?

I was about seven when my mum, Jean, told me I was adopted. It was clearly getting uncomfortable for my parents, as my dad, Ed, managed to look away from his paper and over the top of his specs long enough to notice that my brother Garry, almost three years my junior, was now towering above me.

The stature thing I learned to live with. I have heard all the jokes and the "clever" nicknames fired in my direction down the years – starting with the school ones: Shorty, Titch and the eponymous Lofty. Worse, on some occasions. But it got to the point where I would turn the joke on myself, or even make a virtue of it. There is a never-ending line of self-deprecating gags in my locker, such as: "I get all my clothes at the Build-a-Bear Workshop", with the follow-up: "It is the one place where I can reach the top peg".

There have been swings and roundabouts with being vertically challenged. I used to get passed down to the front at football grounds but have always felt invisible when trying to get served at the bar in a pub. I love those click-and-collect and get-served-at-your-table apps we have now.

Mum and dad were both exiled Londoners, dad from the Surrey border, in Carshalton. Mum had moved to that area with her family after being bombed out of Bermondsey, right opposite the Rotherhithe Tunnel in London's docklands, during the Blitz.

Her dad, James, who died in the awful winter of 1963, worked up in the 'Smoke' in a foundry, while nan, Clare, ran the house and worked part-time as a school cleaner. I recall mum went to her dad's funeral while Garry, my brother, and I stayed at home. The power was cut and I have vivid memories of sitting on my dad's lap at the kitchen table, playing with a US-style black and white police car in the candlelight. How poetic that my youngest brother, now a sherrif's deputy in the States, picked my wife and I up in one at Cincinnati airport one time!

Dad's parents were very different. Grandad Sydney, a Bristolian, was quiet and considered but the life and soul in the pub. Nan Bridget, was Irish Catholic and very dour. She always wore an apron - went to bed in it for all I knew – and the house, on a small green, was always cold. Dad came from a big family with four brothers and a sister who was hard as nails. She had to be - she later lived in Belfast and drove a bus, which she once had to give up when armed terrorists demanded it.

Mum's mum was very, well, mumsy. The sort to lick her hanky and wash any grime off your face while you tried to recoil. She loved her garden and her soil was soot black, which explained why you could grow anything there. Shame she didn't actually plant me there, though. Her house was down the road from St Helier Hospital, which was mistakenly bombed during the war because from the air, it looked like Buckingham Palace.

My folks had resolved to tell me I was adopted as soon as they felt I was able to understand. I recall sitting on mum's knee – I have since grown enough for this to be no longer feasible - with dad in his usual chair by the old fire, before he headed off for a night shift at the bakery up the road from our home in Broadwater Crescent, Stevenage.

I recall him saying little, if anything. It took a while for me to process the news. My world didn't suddenly cave in; far from it. I felt secure as far as I recall – but I did become aware of subtle differences in the way I saw my family and the world around me and there were times in my teens when they were magnified, as most things are.

Mum had lost four babies in pregnancy - it must have been awful. She had given up trying to have one, hence the search to adopt. Later, when she had Garry, and the mite had to have a full blood transfusion at birth.

Even today there are occasional reminders of my past, such as when the doctor asks if there is any history of such-and-such in the family. I usually say: "You tell me, doc... I was adopted". That usually ends the line of conversation abruptly. I always assumed that, no matter your circumstances, that sort of medical information at least would follow you all your life.

I could blame any feelings of difference in my formative years for a series of failed relationships and marriages – but that would be untrue. It was, I think, more down to serious attachment issues that pre-dated my adoption.

Being left for hours by "foster carers" in less than sanitary conditions and contracting dysentery would not have helped, and it hints at a level of serious neglect. I am convinced I had neither the nurture nor nutrition that I needed in my earliest days and that contributed to my lack of stature beyond the influence of my genes. And, having been ignored for long periods, I learned to play quietly on my own and make few demands of others.

I had been given up at birth and was eight months old when mum and dad began fostering me. Mum was not quite old enough, at 24, to formally adopt at that point. But I didn't know any of that – and mum knew very little more of my full story herself – until much later, when I got my records sent to me.

It would actually be more than 50 years, and one failed attempt, before I discovered a larger portion of my personal truth. It arrived in the post when I was living in New Zealand, and came in a red folder retrieved from council social services' archives in Croydon, south London. For years, particularly during those testy, latter teen ones, I wrestled with whether I should try to track down my birth mother. I feared slighting my mum and put the notion to the back of my mind – though I need not have worried. The issue was with me, not her, and we have talked about it openly.

I worried, too, whether I would be appearing to my birth mum like some long-feared ghost; that she might not want me to upset the life she had built for herself, perhaps with a new partner who wasn't aware of any past indiscretions. There may have been immense feelings of guilt or shame on her part; I didn't, couldn't know.

Mum was only party to some of my past – the bits that social services were permitted to mention. I was in local authority care but in hospital with dysentery when she first saw me. It is a disease contracted most likely from a parasite, associated with unclean food or water. It can be deadly in babies. If I cried with pain, dehydration would have meant there were no tears. My file, which I finally received when I was in my early fifties, came with daily temperature charts which showed the infection being tamed gradually, with comments in the margin such as: "Paul had a lovely outing this afternoon in his pram and seems well in himself".

Mum had wanted a baby for some time and had that series of distressing miscarriages. "Adoption was so much easier then," she recalls, "even than when I fostered babies a few years later. There were rules and checks – but they bent the rules as it suited them. You had to be 25 – and 25 years older than the child you were adopting. I pointed out that I'd never be 25 years older than you, but they let that slide.

"The only stipulation from the mother, who was Irish, was that you were to be brought up a Catholic. I wasn't, but Ed was – though he wasn't a practising one. They never followed it up and we moved from Croydon, where we were living, to Stevenage before you were five. Apart from a few outings to Sunday school, and hymns in assembly at school, that was religion done with for you. In the end, it was left to you."

Social services clearly weren't at all concerned where I was to be living: in a flat above a butchers' shop in run-down West Croydon – on the third floor, with no lighting on stairs that were dangerously steep. And the officials clearly never saw the rats that would sometimes venture up the steps, my dad or an uncle beating them away with a broom.

"We really had only one bedroom, the other was for storage," said mum, "and it was so cold. The building had been condemned as uninhabitable and was knocked down soon after we moved. We had the basics and an old butler-style sink that I used to bath you in. It was a rough end of Croydon, with dodgy families and dismantled cars all around.

"A few years before we moved in, Derek Bentley was hanged for the murder of a policeman in a botched burglary in the area." The story was told in a 1991 film, 'Let Him Have It', featuring Christopher Ecclestone and Tom Courtenay. The case turned on the interpretation of the title phrase – which either meant give up the gun, or to use it in anger.

"We were both from Carshalton and had to move away from our parents because the local council refused to house the children of tenants. I never understood that. When we moved to Stevenage, my mum thought it was the other end of the world. It was 30 miles north but we didn't drive and it was a long Green Line bus run."

Mum had wanted a girl and there was only one available when she came to see me at the hospital. "I don't know what had happened to the little girl but she was totally petrified of me. They offered you to us instead and had clearly made an effort – dressing you up in a lovely romper suit. You had a terrible fear of white coats and that stayed with you for a while when we went to see doctors or dentists," she said.

"Because of the age thing, we agreed to take you on a fostered basis. But we had to wait because you had been badly ill and the doctor was on holiday. He had to sign that you were fit and well enough to leave.

And it was all on an understanding that the mother could come in any time in the first six months and take you back – but we weren't worried about that as she'd never had any contact, as far as we were told."

So it was off to Croydon. And those stairs. I fell down them once. "Luckily it was just the bottom three. Any higher and you might not have been here now. The place was a death trap and I could not wait to get out."

Obviously I have few memories of Croydon, though I can picture feeding the ducks at a pond nearby, a big Butler sink in the flat that I used to be bathed in, plus seeing mum do the ironing with it plugged in to a ceiling light socket. Health and Safety would have gone mad.

I did become a minor local celebrity, though. Mum had my picture taken at a nearby photographers, with me standing on a chair while clutching a toy train. I must have been about three or four. The guy colourised it and it was in his shop window for months.

There are a broad range of circumstances in which children can find themselves in care and up for adoption. The mantra trotted out is that all parties act "for the good of the child". What they didn't add back then was that this "good' does not include letting the child in on the secret. There are records in archives but you are not allowed to see them. At least that used to be the case.

Everyone who has been adopted is different with

it. I saw a brilliant interview on YouTube by LBC's James O'Brien with comedian and columnist Mark Steel. Both had been adopted and they described how they hadn't had any desire to find out about their backgrounds until much later. With Mark, it came only when his own son was born and he felt his birth mum might want to know them both.

She had been 19 and lived next door to his aunt, as he has come to know her, in a flat in west London. The girl confessed that she was "in a pickle" and didn't know what to do. "My aunt suggested that, as her brother and his wife in Swanley, Kent, could not have children, perhaps when the baby was born they might take the baby in. This was 1960 and there weren't forms and complicated stuff like that. It was a bit like getting rid of a fridge – you'd have to fill in so many forms to do that now!" said Mark.

He eventually discovered that his mum was living a Bohemian life in Rimini, Italy, and his natural father was French. People would say to him: "Well, that explains why you like cheese!"

"But I didn't have that conversation when I was six – the one where they tell you: 'You're special. You're not like the other children whose mums and dads have to keep them even though they hate the little bastards'."

James made the observation, which had not struck me at all, that when Mark's son Elliot was born, he would have been the first person Mark had met in his life that was a biological relative. So it would be with my daughter, Stefanie, when she arrived in 1990.

Unlike James and Mark, I had a deep-seated, though far from constant need to discover what I had done, merely by being born, that was so awful as to warrant being given up. I imagined all sorts of scenarios, none of them terribly good. When, in my thirties, I first tried to look into my past, to trace my birth mother and any siblings I might have, I ran into a brick wall of officialdom. At the public records' office in London, I could get only so deep before hitting the concrete foundations.

Peter Higgs, the long-time golf and tennis writer at the Mail on Sunday, was also adopted and went through the same process. He was three months old when he was adopted by "teetotal Methodists who were not particularly warm-hearted".

Peter, a colleague for a number of years, said he was incredibly shy and can't remember speaking much to anyone until he was ten. Imagine, then, the ordeal of having to ask a difficult question at a packed press conference.

"I got used to it over the years, but it was an ordeal at times," he said, recalling one particular Wimbledon. Steffi Graf had just won the ladies' singles, and assistant editor Rod Gilchrist had a headline and page waiting – Peter had to try to get her to say she did it for her dad, who had recently been jailed for dodging $7m in tax on her income.

"It was ridiculous. I asked the question and Steffi just put her head in her hands as if to say, 'I've just won this trophy and you have to ask me that!'.

Someone moved the conference on and I didn't get the quote – but Rod ran the story anyway."

I, too, was shy when I was at school. I seldom put my head above the parapet. I hope Higgsy tells his story one day because he has a fund of great inside tales – from being threatened with physical violence by golfer Colin Montgomerie, to being called "Peter Fucking Higgs" by Nick, now Sir Nick, Faldo.

I had my share of threats – and even got banned briefly from covering Stevenage Athletic football games, and bawled out by another club chairman. But more on that later.

Some kids whose confidence might be affected in a subliminal way by being adopted may be quiet but are busy growing thick skins.

Back to the hunt for my birth mother when I was in my early thirties. The best that adopted people could do back then was to take part in some weird 'Guess Who' procedure. You put your name in a register, held in Lytham St Annes, Lancashire, expressing an interest in finding your birth mother – and hoped that she had filled in a corresponding form saying she'd quite like to find you. If a pair of entries matched, you could advance to the next square on the board.

That drew a blank, and I didn't have the resources to hire a private detective, so I gave up. I was in my fifties when I heard that the law had changed. So I tried again.

"Would you like to see your file?" a functionary from the same Somerset House I had emerged from empty-handed so many years before was now able to say It was a remote conversation, though, via email, as I was living 11,000 miles away.

3 To be sure

I've never had a secret thing for Riverdance or Guinness, or even a quiet liking for a Val Doonican cardigan, but it turned out that I was, am, at least half Irish. I will admit to liking Irish films and dramas that feature rugged Emerald Isle coastlines and quirky characters and was a huge fan of Dave Allen.

In fact, the only time have had Guinness was in recovery from a football injury. I don't mean the usual post-match bevvy of a Sunday lunchtime. I got assaulted, in truth, suffering a damaged pancreas, and was in hospital for a week, right through Christmas.

The doctor said I had lost a bit of weight (I was 9st wet most of my younger life) and recommended a touch of the Liffey water to aid my recovery at home. He stopped short of sticking it on prescription. But I could actually see my flat from my hospital bed. I digress again – must be the Irish in me.

The big, red folder that I was sent in New Zealand unlocked a number of "secrets", starting with my mother's full name: Bridget Mary Hughes.

She was a domestic, who lived at 13 Rupert Gardens, Lambeth, London SW9, which is sandwiched between Camberwell and Brixton. Not the most salubrious area. There was no mention of a father, though two possibles were hinted at in some accompanying paperwork from a social services interview with her. One more and I could have had a starring role in Mamma Mia! How funny it would have been if Piers Brosnan was my dad after all. I could be 003 and a half. Or Premium Bond

One "candidate" worked at offices in Soho where Bridget – known as Bridie to her friends – cleaned, while the other was a travelling salesman "from the West Country or Wales". She had a brother living in the Principality, so there could have been a vague connection.

The idea of being conceived on an office desk in Shaftesbury Avenue appeals to my sense of humour – and perhaps hints that I was set to be pursuing desk jobs all my career. I was born at St Giles Hospital, Camberwell – which just about makes me a proper Cockney, too. Would you Adam and Eve it?

The hospital had its origins in the Camberwell Workhouse Infirmary and was hit by a V1 bomb during World War Two. The hospital closed in 1983 and it seems the flats in Rupert Gardens were knocked down, too, and rebuilt after Bridget moved away.

My file contained just one small, scribbled note in her own scrawl, saying that I had been handed over complete with two vests, two pairs of socks, a couple of babygrows and a cardigan. I have always travelled light...

Bridie, I discovered, had been brought up on a farm in Mullyamley, Co Cavan. It was so remote that the address was given as 'care of Corlismore Post Office'. Spelling mistakes in my documentation suggested that her accent was quite broad Irish and slowed my online search for the place. It is not far from the county town of Cavan and close to the Northern Ireland border – but there is little there apart from farms, with tight lanes and tall hedgerows. It is an Ulster county but actually across the border in the Republic.

I knew nothing of her story then, or of how she came to be in London. But she presumably wanted to see if there was more to life than stoking peat fires and tending cattle, some of which actually lived in a part of the house at times. Downstairs, of course. Upstairs would be just weird. The other big find was that I had elder siblings, John and Mary. I was able to trace Mary online as she hadn't married, by her surname, Priest. So ... I could have been a half-Irish Priest. And they have not exactly had the best press in recent years...

From those details came a phone number – then an overseas call to Mary in south Yorkshire. She was, as you would expect, shocked to hear from me – but I sensed not entirely surprised. She said: "I heard there might be another child – but I thought it was a girl."

John was more dubious at first. But you only had to see us together to see a strong physical resemblance.

It later transpired that there was indeed a girl: Margaret, who lives in Cornwall. She, like me, had been given up for adoption.

When I came back to the UK in 2005, I met Mary in Doncaster. It was a strange but wonderful experience. I would say she was like the sister I never had – except that I did have a sister, and I just never knew about it. Mary broke the news to me that Bridget had long since died

She had lived in Ilford, Essex, with a new partner, Bill. She was hit by a car while she was on a zebra crossing and never properly got over her injuries.

She died on Boxing Day, 1990. Mary hated Christmas ever since. By all accounts Bridie was a lively, outgoing woman, with lots of friends, and always happy to stop for a gossip.

Given that I was by now in my fifties, I had already resigned myself to the fact she was likely to have died, so there was not the huge feeling of disappointment you might expect. I had the compensation of another brother – making three – and two sisters. I was told that Bridget had two brothers in Ireland, Pat and Paul, both farmers, though Mary did not know if either was still alive.

Mary recounted how, as kids, she and John would go over to stay on the farm for the summer holidays. John remembers seeing piles of unopened cheques lying around – farm subsidy payments from the EEC (now the EU) – and they would only get paid in many months later. It didn't seem a prosperous operation and there was little social life there, so they could see why Bridget moved away to London.

Bridie and her husband John were living in Lambeth with John (junior) and Mary, when she broke the news that she was expecting me... and that he was not the father. He gave her an ultimatum: she could keep me, but if she did she would have to leave without John and Mary. The enormity of that choice struck me; I immediately had enormous sympathy for her dilemma. It was an unfair and impossible choice – and did leave me thinking it possible that she had sometimes spared a thought for me and, indeed, Margaret.

I wondered, too, if my father ever had any idea that he was a dad, or was merely happy he hadn't been left to foot the bill. Or, indeed, whether Bridie ever saw him again.

In idle moments commuting, half in a trance, on the Tube, I had sometimes looked across at the person sitting opposite me and wondered if they might be my brother or sister. There was an even more fleeting fantasy that I might have been someone like Richard Branson's little, lost secret. But while I might have liked the idea of owning a Caribbean is-land, I have never felt compelled to sue the NHS for not being given a lucrative contract, so I ruled that one out..

From speaking to John and Mary, it was clear that I definitely had the better end of the deal. When their parents split, they eventually chose to go with their father... the best of a bad job. Bridget's new partner, Bill, was unpredictable and violent. She had met in Ilford where they were both working, cleaning trains.

My siblings and their feckless father were running from ever mounting debts. There were a few dodgy midnight flits – and none of today's credit-checking databases to hound their trail. But the pattern kept repeating and they moved further northwards, to Peterborough for a time, and ended up in Doncaster.

John is slightly taller than me but of similar build. He is six years older, Mary was four years my senior.

John had worked for a time down the mines in Yorkshire but didn't stay long. He told how he once fell asleep at the junction of two linked conveyor belts, allowing coal to back up and block the exits. But he painted a grim picture of life in the pits – one he was thankful to escape as soon as he could.

He later worked as a delivery driver for the coun-cil until being overcome with nerve pain and had to retire on ill health. He married Mary's school friend, Gwen, and they have grown-up children and grand-children, and live in a smart semi on the edge of

Doncaster.

John told of the fights he had with his abusive, drunken father – once knocking him through a wall. So he didn't have many fond memories of his childhood, and losing out on his schooling meant that he is not great at reading and writing. But he is worldly-wise, if not academic, and holds strong opinions.

The constant moves in their youth led to them changing schools often – Mary said she had no fewer than three in one academic year. When I heard this, I admitted to feeling guilty at having had such a stable upbringing, in schools that were still fairly new, well equipped and with very good teachers. But I don't think either of them were envious of me or the life chances I had.

Mary worked as a domestic in a private care home, 100 yards along the street from her small but tidy bungalow in Edlington, a former pit village, with her much-loved Patterdale terrier, Pepsi, and they would go on long walks, often Bridlington or Clee-thorpes, a shortish drive away. She retired soon after we met. The long shifts and lack of staff had been punishing and she was glad to get out.

Mary told me she was gay and had lost her long-term partner, Jill, a few years earlier, to cancer. She had a close friend, Eileen, but was clearly quite a lonely person. She had looked about online but said how difficult it was in your sixties to meet some-one, let alone another gay person. She and John were close, too, I suspect from their traumatic youth, and

Mary struck me as being emotionally strong and similarly smart from a tough upbringing.

A couple of years after I met John and Mary, Margaret popped up. She, too, had been searching for her roots. She lives near Newquay but had previously had a home in Norfolk. She was on her own and had moved after losing a son in a road accident. We had a few 'team' meetings – including a great party in Wellingborough, Northants, where I was living at the time.

They filled me in with stories of my birth mother, as did Bernadette, the daughter of Bridie's friend for more than 40 years. Bernie is Irish, too, and they were kindred spirits. They got to know each other at work, in the car industry. Bernie, who lives in Seven Kings, near Ilford, says she and Bridie were inseparable. "I always saw her as a sister. She was the life and soul and I have never laughed as much since she died.

"She had a terrible life with her second partner, Bill. He was violent and very controlling. She never had any money of her own - even though she inherited a house in from an old man she had cared for. Towards the end she took the old feller into her own home to nurse him and he left his big, four-bed place to her plus some cash as a thank-you.

"I remember one day pulling up at some traffic lights and seeing Bill in the next car to us with a girlfriend. It didn't surprise Bridie when I told her – but she insisted on going home. Next morning she turned up at my house at about 3am, all black and blue, and I insisted she moved in with me. She was the sort of person who would give you her last shilling and I would have done anything for her.

"She got hit by a car on a crossing one day and was seriously ill. She never really recovered and her health suffered for a good few years before she died one Christmas, aged 73. It always casts a bit of a shadow over the festive time.

"Bridie was very religious and would call in at St Peter and St Paul when she was going by. I think she had a thing for the priest! But Bill was not going to hold a service for her after she died and I went mad at him. He changed his mind and I was pleased about that. It is what she would have wanted.

"But he was a b****** to her. When she was ill they moved her from hospital back home to a bed in her living room. Bill wouldn't move the sofa, so she couldn't even see the TV from her bed. It was cruel.

"At the funeral, Johnny sat at the back. If he had been any closer, he'd have killed Bill. Bill took all her money and controlled who she saw – splitting her away from Johnny and Mary. I used to tell him and so did Cathy, our other great friend, who is also Irish.

Bridie had a very hard life but she always had this big smile and was always trying to have a laugh. We were all the very best of friends and my kids loved their aunty Bridie. She always had time for them."

Bernie's daughter, also named Bernadette, recalls Bridie stealing her takeaway Chinese every week. "My boyfriend used to order extra. It was every Saturday night at our house, Bridie with her glass of whiskey. Everybody loved her and my youngest daughter is named after her.

"I remember when she died, me and mum collected her ashes, which her brother John took back to Ireland to put on her mother's grave."

In 2015, Mary was diagnosed with advanced ovarian cancer. It was around the time I had just been made redundant and we visited her often in Doncaster Infirmary. She chose to go home for her final days. They set up a bed in her living room and it was a pitiful sight. A very slight lady, she was even more frail at the end.

One of her wishes when she was ill had been to visit Stratford-upon-Avon. My wife Pam and I go there often from our home in Leicester, sometimes just for an evening. It is always uplifting to be down by the river and we time our outings to miss the hordes of trippers and tour buses. Mary had never been and we had talked about her being well enough for us to drive her there for a day out – but, sadly, it didn't happen.

On her birthday or close to the anniversary of her death, we leave flowers for her down by the river, usually against a tree near the plaque marking the life of Vivien Leigh, which is on the green outside the Royal Shakespeare Theatre. The inscription to Leigh reads: "A lass unparalleled".

That's how I like to remember my big sis. It felt like I had lost her all over again.

4 School days

There are turning points throughout your life and some can be very profound. I remember two big ones from my school days. The first was at junior school, in Stevenage, when my teacher, Mr Pullen, believed that I could get into grammar school with a bit of a push on my English (which probably comes as no surprise to some work colleagues down the years). The other was when I messed up my O-Levels but was fortunate to be given a second chance. That was the making of me.

Mr Pullen must have been in his early 60s, perhaps older, and was a largely unsmiling chap who wore fawn-coloured knitted cardigans with large brown buttons on them. He had a hearing-aid and it was not unknown for us to play up to it, in Fawlty Towers' Mrs Richards fashion... only without the hordes of wildebeest sweeping by majestically. But he certainly worked his magic for me: my English improved sufficiently and I got that leg-up – though Nobel was only a Grammar for the first two years that I was there.

He brought many of our lessons alive – who knew geology could engage a 10-year-old? Well, it did feature lots of dinosaurs, and we learned the difference between Triassic and Jurassic. We did wonder if he'd witnessed it all in person. He'd tell us that if we did geography at secondary school, we might get to go on exciting field trips. Well, those oxbow lakes don't build themselves... do they?

My school report gave me an overall A-minus and my Maths was marginally better than my English. I preferred kicking a football almost every waking hour to reading a book at home. Mr Pullen wrote in my report: "One of the younger members of the class, Paul works quietly and well, achieving satisfactory results."

A year earlier, Mrs Flook noted that I was "a quiet boy who works industriously, though rather slowly" but "a helpful member of class". I think they call that being damned with faint praise.

My memories of the first couple of years at Roebuck are of lots of sunny days with some lessons held outside on the grass. There were fewer in the latter two years, when our classroom was one of a couple of speedily thrown-up wooden huts – probably ex-military – with the main buildings, barely a decade old, unable to cope with a swiftly-rising roll of pupils. They were cold. The girls would huddle against the radiators during the breaks, and rain hammering on the roof meant you had to shout to be heard. I bet they all have piles now!

I vividly remember a lesson with Mr Deakin in my second year, when we had to listen to a classical music track, I think it was Grieg, and write about what it brought to mind. I remember none of what I actually penned – and, yes, it was nib and ink then, with spidery handwriting that should have had me pegged as a future doctor. But he singled out my prose for its "imagination". I tended to fly under the radar so I was uncomfortable to be the centre of attention. Nevertheless, it gave me a big lift at the time. Perhaps it planted a seed.

We learned skills such as basket weaving – ideal for those whose career path might not follow the straight and narrow. We didn't go the whole hog and do mail bags, though.

These were the pre-Thatcher days when we still had free school milk and, as I loved the stuff, I'd be straight in for a spare if someone was off sick. Sometimes it was orange juice in the same shaped glass bottles, and I lapped that up, too.

The infants' school was next door and I learned more about the place only long after I left. I do remember the hymns in assembly, questionable school dinners (the chocolate cornflakes and pink custard was the only salavtion), dancing round the Maypole and having to hold a girl's hand as we walked in two neat files to the gate after school each day to be reunited with our mums. Yuk...

Dad, a baker by trade, used to make and donate a huge wheatsheaf-patterned flat loaf for the harvest festival each year. And it would be proudly displayed at morning assembly. That was one up on the kids who brought some out-of-date tinned rhubarb, prunes or wilting veg.

I vividly remember one teacher – the gruff Mrs Woodruff – but warmed to her hugely when I was at college and went back to do work experience. The oddest thing was having the teachers talking to me like an adult – it felt so naughty. I even held back momentarily before I went into the staff room at break times for a cuppa, as that didn't quite seem right either. Nor did calling teachers I knew from before by their first names. I enjoyed working with the kids but never seriously thought of teaching as a career. I was set on my path and was just covering my bases.

One infants' school episode mum couldn't forget was the annual Christmas play one year. I was to be some make-up-the-numbers person – a sentry or something. But Dick Whittington got stage fright minutes before the curtain went up and it seemed the show would have to be cancelled. They asked us for a volunteer to stand in as Dick and nobody came forward. I meekly raised my hand. At this point, some who know me will be saying - 'stand-in Dick... that's about right'.

But there was mum, sitting towards the back of the hall (dad was at work), completely aghast as I shuffled to the front, black 'cat' in tow. The cat's name was Elizabeth and it is possible she was my first crush in a kind of sweet Love Actually way without the drumming. A teacher had to kneel at the front of the stage, in the dark, and feed me whispered lines. I got through it to wild applause, and I think it was mentioned in the local paper, but was happy to retire from the stage at the top. Tom Cruise and Danny deVito had the field for the vertically challenged to themselves.

The school, which is close to the Stevenage football stadium in Broadhall Way, has since been blitzed and modernised and now has prison-like security, with big spiked gates and keypad entry system. It seems so alien to my carefree days there. I have walked past there many times on the way to matches and thought back fondly to my time at school. My whole life was ahead of me, after all.

But soon it was time to make the step up to 'big school' – and another big life-turning point.

5 Nobel

F ew of my junior school chums moved up with me to Nobel and I had to get a bus there each day, so it was all very different and new. It didn't overly faze, me though. It did seem odd wandering around classrooms to each new lesson rather than staying in one place. And it was odd to have the sixth-form girls patting me on the head and say, 'isn't he cute!' as I walked about in my shorts when all the other lads had long trousers.

The bigger shock was for mum, finding out that had we lived 200 yards down the hill towards my junior school the bus ride would have been just over three miles and she wouldn't have had to stump up for the 6d each way fares. She was doubtless thrilled when I later started cycling to and from school each day.

One of Stevenage's best features has always been its purpose-built cycle tracks, walkways and under-passes, which keep you well away from the roads, so mum never had to worry about me getting to school safely on my red bike with drop handlebars that I'd fixed on it instead of the uncool straight ones it came with. It had a rack on the back for my school satchel and Spurs gym bag that often smelled quite strong from days-old damp swim-ming kit or towel. The school rugby shirts were thick and reversible. The normal way, you'd see the blue with a big gold hoop; inside out there was no hoop. That's how we had inter-house matches. I was in Stuart – we had Tudor, Stuart, Hanover and Windsor.

I'd venture to school and back with Andy Wilkin-son, who sported a kind of Blackadder Series One pudding-bowl haircut, and he'd regale me with tales of Monty Python, which his family watched on TV but mine didn't. There was no need for a video, thanks to Andy – not that we knew what one of those was – as he parroted back the previous night's highlights. I did later buy the Python LP, complete with the Silly Walks, Dead Parrot and Four York-shiremen sketches which I shared with like-minded friends – all too often. Lines from the Life of Brian and Holy Grail even now get dropped into our conversations such as the Holy Hand-grenade of Antioch scene. Well, that was one very scary rabbit.

Andy's dad was headmaster of Shephall Manor, a residential school for children with behavioural problems. In 1542, George Nodes, Sergeant of the Buckhounds to Henry VIII, was granted the manor, and his family held it for 250 years. It is a striking building, with extensive grounds that have been nibbled away down the years, and has tennis courts (which we used), plus a warren of rooms, passageways and staircases. It housed orphaned Polish children from 1949 to 1954. My brother Kevin, nine years my junior, became good friends with the daughter of a later head teacher at the school, so he got the repeat experience.

Mick Geraghty was one of the few to go to Nobel from my class at Roebuck and he was the target of pranks which I would say now crossed the line into bullying. 'Carrots' was a soft target. They would dangle his satchel out of our top-floor classroom window or, most famously, wedge him in a square metal bin, which they lifted on top of the teacher's desk one break time and retreated as they waited for her to come in. Heavens knows what she made of it. There was a brief clamour for the guilty parties to come forward – but to no avail.

Mick, who was of a similar stature to me, was quick-tongued and frequently answered back, which probably singled him out, while I kept my head down and avoided the flak. He lived opposite the Our Mutual Friend pub, opposite his house, and where I worked a few evenings a week when I was at college. I was at least able then to repay him for taking some of the crap I might have received. He'd drink light and bitter and I'd make sure he always had a near-pint of bitter and a bottle of light to go with it.

Changing from junior to secondary can be stressful and, when I went to the transfer open evening at Nobel, the head, Leslie Rose, told us boys we would play rugby in the autumn term and then football in winter. I whispered to my dad that, having looked round the room at the size of the lads I'd be playing against, I wondered if I could just do football instead.

Dad, never the diplomat, actually mentioned this to the head afterwards. Mr Rose told me rugby was "important in building character". I thought no more of it – until I found I had been picked for the school team in the first match, against Heathcote... as hooker, in the centre of the scrum. It's normally a position for a bruiser, not a blood donor, I estimated.

When we got ready for the first scrum, my feet dangled freely as I clung, jelly-legged, between the chunky props to either side of me. And, when we locked heads with the opposition front row, it felt like every bone in my body was about to crack and shatter. I never got into the team again – but it was a salutary lesson.

I liked Jim Skipper, our PE teacher. He was as far removed from the cartoonish PE teacher in the movie

'Kes' as you could imagine. While Brian Glover famously acted out the fantasy that he was Bobby Charlton, Mr Skipper had actually played football to a very decent standard. and made nothing of it. He was in a team picture I unearthed in the school library – of Pegasus, who reached an FA Amateur Cup final, I think in 1951. They beat Bishop Auckland 2-1 at Wembley. It was not something he ever mentioned and, I don't know why, but I never brought it up with him. It is a pity, as it would have been a very colourful tale, I am sure.

Pegasus was a team of Oxbridge types managed by people who went on to make a name for themselves in the professional game, including Arthur Rowe, who led Tottenham to the old First Division title in the early fifties with his famed "Push and Run" tactics.

I did play football a couple of times for the school, cricket too, and ran cross country after finishing in the top six in the inter-house event – most likely because many others took odd detours to avoid the muddy course that took in streams now long since refashioned into the Fairlands Lakes complex, which is a haven for sailors, canoeists and anglers.

But it was at chess that I excelled. Aged 11, I was in the top five or six at school, based on a league ladder we had in a lunch-time club, and I played many times for Nobel, including in the national Sunday Times tournament, with matches that took us to nearby towns such as Hitchin and St Albans. Most of the six-player team were sixth formers. As we decamped from the school minibus we must have looked like a University Challenge team with their mascot in tow.

Mr Offa, who ran the chess club until he left when the school ceased to be a grammar, was a brilliant chess tutor. He set up a coaching programme for us and you had to checkmate him in so many moves with a combination of pieces to pass each test to go on to the next level. Proper coaching – I can't think of many places where you would get that, not in the state sector at least.

I'd been playing since I was about eight, when my neighbour, Steven Board, taught me, and the game came easily to me. I loved setting traps three or four moves down the line and watch people fall into them. I'm not sure that kind of thinking permeated other parts of my life. I was sad that the club disbanded with Mr Offa's departure at the end of my second year, though I did "inherit" one of the club's nice chess sets. I'd struggle to beat a computer now at even a basic level and will never know how far I might have progressed had Mr Offa – who we nicknamed "Bamber" for his resemblance to the University Challenge host Bamber Gascoigne – stayed on.

There was a play scheme in the park pavilion in the school holidays and I used to always win the chess and draughts competitions. Once, as a fun stunt, I played six simultaneous chess games, walking up and down the line to make my moves – and beat all six opponents.

Nobel was a "technical grammar": the idea was

that it would turn out kids for apprenticeships in local firms such as British Aerospace, Kodak, ICI and ICL, as well as to feed others on to higher education. So we had wood and metalwork and technical drawing. I was rubbish at them all and probably a danger to myself with the tools they let us loose with.

With hindsight, it would have been handy to have been taught plumbing, electrics and decorating – far more practical for an era when you were still allowed to wire a plug. I've fitted kitchens at home but never needed a lathe – just a plumber to bail me out when faced with a tricky U-bend or leaking hot tap connection.

I did manage to make a chessboard in woodwork. It had clear and yellow Perspex inlaid squares, mounted on a box fashioned from oak. It was a half-decent effort but took me at least a couple of terms to finish. I also made a fruit bowl that I fashioned on the lathe and which mum had for years. Well, one good turn deserves another.

When my brother Garry joined me at Nobel, I was in the third year and he was in the first comprehensive cohort. One of the changes for them was that the boys did a term of cookery and the girls would have a go at woodwork or metalwork. When he left school he did briefly work as a hotel chef. But he worked most of his career at John Lewis, supervising deliveries.

As someone who could benefit from some time reading Delia Smith's "How to Boil an Egg", it is a pity I didn't get a crack at that to build some culinary basics. It would also have meant escaping the risk of an aerial bombardment of flying blackboard rubbers and chalk from our rather brutally impatient technical drawing teacher.

The sciences, geography, history and German interested me most and we had a couple of great school trips supposedly to enhance our understanding of all those subjects – to Hamelin, famed for its Pied Piper, and later to Salzburg, Mozart's birthplace and the backdrop for The Sound of Music.

On that first tip we visited Hanover, with its links to our monarchy, and had a guided tour of a Volkswagen factory – then there was a swimming match with the Hanover club which, given that in the event of a lifesaving exercise I would be the brick, I had intended to watch from the stands.

I had only recently passed my 25 yards – and still don't know how I achieved even that, having been traumatised when I was seven by someone who pushed me under the water in my first school swimming lesson at the town pool. Yet when it came to seeing the school fielding an empty lane because nobody volunteered for the breaststroke, a strange force made me put my hand up. Yet there was no cat to impress this time. Perhaps because they hate water, except when drinking from the kitchen tap.

I used to laugh at the lifesaving awards - kids had to make a liferaft out of their pyjamas and fetch a rubber brick from the bottom of the pool. Both were scenarios I never intended to get involved with out of choice.

My misgivings about the race were great – and doubled when I found that it was a 50m pool. That was twice my lifetime best distance. While the other competitors took off from their blocks and left me in their choppy wake, I started from in the water, pushing off from the side. In racing parlance, I was tailed off at the start – but received some hearty encouragement and then sympathetic applause when I eventually made it to the other end in a slowest all-comers' record that probably still stands. Not the best sporting performance by an Englishman abroad.

I actually felt like that bloke who dresses as deep-sea diver or as Big Ben and finishes the London Marathon just as the marker cones and litter are being collected by some burly blokes perched on the back of a moving truck at sundown. My swimming teacher looked at me in a new light when we got home but I never really warmed to it. I'm sure they named them "infinity pools" because that's how long it would take me to get to the far end. I much prefer being on an inflatable with a cold drink – or just admiring the water from a sun-lounger.

A couple of years later, we were in Salzburg, an impressive medieval Austrian city dominated from on high by a huge schloss (castle) and the towering Tyrolean mountains. It is a place I would love to revisit for its more cultural offerings – we teen lads preferred to inhabit the bierkellers, despite us all being underage and not very tolerant of strong ale. The steins were bigger than me.

We had an outing to the nearby saltmines, which we explored while sitting one behind the other on long, wooden slides, in full "Oops Upside Your Head" mode – and got a look up to the Berchtesgaden, Hitler's mountain-top "Wolf's Lair" retreat.

These trips must have been a strain on the family budget, especially with another Fry in the household, Kevin having arrived in 1965. Mum by now worked part-time in the greengrocer's down the road, opposite where she now lives, in sheltered accommodation.

Eventually there came the exams and, while I did plenty of cramming, it clearly never went in. I had been expected to do much better than finish with just two O-Levels – geography and physics-with-chemistry – and CSE equivalents in English and Maths. It would have closed a lot of doors to me had that been that. And yet I was more numb, perhaps in shock, than disappointed.

In my defence, I had been crippled by hayfever in a couple of exams, as they were inexplicably cutting the grass outside, with the windows to the hall fully open as the sun belted down. In one test in particular, my eyes were itching so terribly and streaming that I could not see the paper for a while. I lost at least a quarter of the allotted two hours before being able to see any question clearly. I should have said something to the invigilator or to my teacher afterwards, but I didn't, thinking that was just it... tough.

I don't know the exact sequence of events that followed that summer but, after I received my results in August, I was involved in a conversation with, I think, my form tutor and my dad. The school gave us the offer for me to repeat the entire year, rather than just do some autumn exam re-sits. They said I had been one of the youngest in the intake and was not far short of being in the following school year anyway.

The Education Act has a provision for such instances, recognising that children develop at different rates and can have wildly varying abilities, even within the same school year, depending on whether they were born in September or, like me, the following August.

I agreed to the idea and admit that I had some feelings of apprehension at dropping down a year. I feared being labelled as a failure. But I never experienced any such comments, at least not to my face. I made friends quickly, losing my dinner money to them at a game of cards that first lunch break. That immediately cut me some slack.

I won much of it back in the ensuing weeks, but not in an obvious way...

In many ways that lower year felt a better fit. At the end of it, with the exams out of the way, I even went on a barge holiday on the Thames with seven of the lads – four of us on each boat. That was memorable for one particular morning when I was asked to push off the side of a lock, only for the thing to move away suddenly and leave me groping in mid-air before slipping underneath the vessel. At least those swimming lessons had finally come in handy. When I finally bobbed up, I was filthy. The Thames wasn't the cleanest – there was a thin film of oil on the surface, and goodness knows what else. I was at least able to give the hull a quick inspection, though.

We tied up one night in Teddington, on our way to our intended destination, Windsor, and went in search of a pub. In the first one we came across, a big place, were a bit taken aback to find that all the beer glasses were plastic - which was a new thing then, and the bar was packed only with men. We had stumbled, with no warning, on a strippers' night. I can't say that we made our excuses and left – neither can I get the image of that snake out of my head whenever I hear Eric Clapton's "I Shot the Sheriff". It must have been a pain in the asp for the lady in question, too.

I am still in touch with people from both my fifth years. One from the lower year, Dave Pickard, was a Sunday league team-mate, our goalkeeper, for a good few seasons. Indeed, with the passing of time it has become a bit blurred as to which friend was in which year.

I would imagine that staying back a year is much harder now in terms of the bullying kids get, especially out of hours over social media. We never put insulting notes through kids' letterboxes took photos of our dinner - because it took so long to get the images back from the developers, –even if you did get the bonus of the free film to replace the one you had ruined with all the missing heads and feet and gurning.

For me, though, that year was an enriching experience, allowing me time to grow up, widening my circle of friends and preparing me for a lifetime of change. New jobs and house moves have not fazed me as much as they might have done had I stayed on that intended track.

It had been a matter of feeling awkward for a few days, then staying focused on the end result – 10 O-levels, with some improved grades and the chance to go to college, far better equipped to succeed.

When I got in touch recently with Barry Burningham, a current teacher at Nobel, to check if there were any surviving records of my time there and asked how unusual it was for a pupil to repeat the O-levels year, as I knew nobody else who had, he said: "It's not so rare as you might think – I did it myself."

6 New Town

The older I get, the more I appreciate having been brought up in Stevenage. It is often derided as an antiseptic new town, full of roundabouts, concrete buildings and the great unwashed who were bombed out of London in World War II but it was conceived as a safe, happy environment for families – and life in the 1960s and 1970s was largely what the town's post-war creators imagined and promised.

There is an element of rose-tinteds, sure, but as a social experiment it was a success. It has been busy reinventing itself of late with a £1bn transformation programme. Strange that it would start again you may think, after barely 80 years – but it has the luxury of being able to do so, unlike many other places.

The area has a rich history of Roman and Saxon life but Stevenage's prosperity came from the Great North Road, which was turnpiked in the early 18th century. Many inns in the High Street served the 21 stagecoaches that passed through each day in 1800. There were so many pubs and bars that a rite of passage as we hit our late teens was to have a pint in as many as possible in a single night (it never ended well for the small car showroom at the far end of the High Street).

In November 1946, Stevenage was chosen as the site of the first 'New Town', one of eight in the Greater London area, each providing housing for 60,000 people. There are more than 80,000 there now.

The existing locals hated the idea and protested, dubbing the town 'Silkingrad', after John Silkin, the Minister for Housing. "It's no good your jeering, it's going to be done," he told noisy objectors at one meeting in what was left as the Old Town.

Six neighbourhoods were planned, each with 10,000 homes, its own community centre, pub, shops and doctors' surgery. Stevenage would be the first to have a fully-pedestrianised town centre and separate industrial area.

The first residents moved there in 1952 - you could get a house so long as you had already found work. Local amenities were slower in setting up and those pioneering residents had to use mobile shops or walk the mile or so to Old Stevenage, where the railway station was located then, partly through the mud on unmade roads.

We lived at 210 Broadwater Crescent, a three-bedroom mid-terrace which was covered in pebbledash front and back. We were not the first occupants but everything would have seemed like new to my parents after that condemned flat in Croydon.

We had the Tuck family on one side, and the Ivorys on the other, and my parents socialised with both families. Rose Tuck, whose family were from a village near Gibraltar, became more like a sister to mum and she was most selfless person I have met. She was widowed for more than 30 years after her Bill died from a brain tumour, and yet she never complained about her own growing list of ailments. Even in her 80s she was still pushing the bins out for neighbours who were fit and in their 30s.

Their kids, Gerald, Mercedes, Lisa and Bill, have been more like family, though I don't see them much now.

The other side of the Ivorys were Harry and Marge Board and son Steven, who was my biggest playmate for a good few years. His dad was always building stuff and put together a brilliant table football game for us – with goals and nets, and wooden players on bars, all cut, sanded and painted, half in Arsenal colours, Steve's team, and the other team as Spurs, mine. We played that for hours. Steve also taught me chess with a clay set Harry had made and painted, the pieces in green or yellow glaze.

I remember playing cricket with him in the park - just the two of us – I just could not bowl him out. The faster I steamed in, the further Steve hit it into the woods behind me. It was all the more amazing since he'd had a problem with his legs when he was very young and had to wear a metal calliper on one for a good few years.

I lost touch with Steve when he went to Alleyne's Boys Grammar in the Old Town and I went to Nobel, a mixed grammar at the other end of town. Then we both moved away after school and further educa- tion. But our paths did cross unexpectedly a couple of times.

There was one famous night in 1971 when Spurs were playing Arsenal, with the Gunners looking to emulate the League and Cup Double which Totten- ham had achieved exactly a decade earlier.

The match was a sell-out - with an estimated 40,000 locked outside. Incredibly, I bumped into Steve and his dad outside in the Paxton Road end – none of us were able to get in and my mate Paul Cork and his dad George and I had to settle for the radio commentary on the drive back home. And, more than 20 years later, I bumped into Steve in a car park at Porlock, in Somerset. I had taken a chance detour there on my way back from Devon, meeting friends.

The children in our row of houses all went to Roe- buck Juniors but then took mostly separate paths for secondary school. Between 1955 and 1965, a new school opened In Stevenage almost every year and, in 1962, the A1(M) bypass was built. Cynics joke that it was the best thing about the town.

In 1961, the Locarno Ballroom opened and hosted The Rolling Stones, Tom Jones and Jimmy Hendrix, among others. My former sports editor, Kit Galer's band, Kit and the Saracens, appeared on bills with Lulu and The Who. In my teen years, the venue became the Mecca ballroom, replete with pints of Watney's bitter, girls dancing around their handbags, throbbing disco music, strobe lights and glitterballs – and some very strange fashions.

I was definitely a victim, with my cream, 16-inch bottomed trousers, tight at the top end, and bright canary yellow or crimson round-collared shirts and platform shoes. The built-up shoes didn't do me any favours, I worked out years later. I might have grown three or four inches perched on top of them – but then so had everyone on theirs, stunting any closing of the stature gap.

I was still a short arse. And the girls wore heels. There were all too few slow dances for me at the end of the night and too many solo walks home from town for me. I was painfully shy, which didn't help – though perhaps, on reflection, my dress sense did not help. I wasn't alone, mind.

With hindsight, my brother Garry would now be considered the coolest, with his liking for the Davids – Bowie, and Gilmour – and Barry White. I oscillated between Status Quo and Earth, Wind and Fire, which was a stretch.

It could be quite a long, stuttering walk back from the Mecca as I chose to save the taxi money so that I could go with Corky to watch Tottenham Hotspur matches. The actual length of the walk correlated quite closely with the amount I'd had to drink.

I never felt threatened on my 2am walks – in fact, I recall barely ever seeing anyone on the streets, except for the occasional policeman, who was usually walking with his bike beside him, though I don't recall ever being challenged.

A new swimming pool was welcomed not just by the locals but by the majority of the schools in town and beyond that didn't have their own pool, as we did at Nobel. Golfer Sir Nick Faldo, who grew up in nearby Welwyn Garden City, was a Hertfordshire breaststroke champion and held records at Stevenage pool that stood for many years. He also had a crack at cycling before settling on golf as his chosen sport.

In 1972, a Leisure Centre was built which included the Gordon Craig Theatre, and not long afterwards came a council-run golf course designed by John Jacobs, which was indeed a cracker. It was where I bought my first set of clubs, Petron Impalas, and learned to play, albeit never that well. It was often the famed great walk spoiled, but I enjoyed it all the same.

The range of sports facilities in Stevenage - as well as those in schools and some of the town's biggest employers, such as British Aerospace – helped the town punch well above its weight in sporting terms. Stevenage boasts two world champions, though you may have only heard of one of them – F1 star Lewis Hamilton.

The other is Tim Spears, the 2008 world landyacht champion. If it seems improbable that a place with no beach could produce such a talent, you can add Alan Munro to the list. As a jockey he won both the Derby and Irish Derby - and there isn't a Thoroughbred stables for miles.

Former England cricketer Roland Butcher grew up in the town, as did footballers Ashley Young, Kevin Phillips, Ian Allinson, Jason Shackell and Jimmy Gilligan; so too football referee Graham Poll, and Ryder Cup golfer Ian Poulter - a Stevenage schoolboy and later apprentice pro at the nearby Family Golf Centre in Graveley, on the old A1 just north of town.

You can add one-time motorcycle speedster George Brown. He worked for Vincent, who made bikes in the town until 1955. Stevenage has always lauded its sporting and cultural heroes and there is a brilliant mural of local folk made good, on the walkway through the leisure centre, connecting the railway station and town centre. There is even an Olympic gold medallist on the list – 800m runner Tom Hampson, who was a Stevenage development corporation official later in life after his success in Los Angeles in 1932.

The New Town was the backdrop for the 1968 teen angst movie, 'Here We Go Round the Mulberry Bush'. Based on a Hunter Davies novel, it starred Barry Evans, Judy Geeson, Denholm Elliott, Diane

Keen, Christopher Timothy, Angela Scoular and Nicky Henson. It followed the sexploits of teenager Jamie McGregor (Evans) in the permissive society of the 60s. Locals can still recognise many of the little-altered locations used in the film, such as the Joy-ride platform and town centre pond, fountain and clocktower. My old school, Nobel, featured, too.

In recent years, the town's growth – from 60,000 to 80,000-plus – has seen it fall to the modern scourge of multiple car ownership. The car is king. Parking has narrowed the main estate roads and clogged side streets, while there has a been a lot of infill housing, making the place feel more claustro-phobic than when I grew up there.

Hugely controversially, more land has been grabbed to expand the town, including a part de-scribed as "the loveliest in England" by novelist EM Forster. In 1883, when he was four, author Edward Morgan Forster moved to Rooks Nest – a Grade I-listed home where much later he penned his novel 'Howard's End'. The area will soon have 800 homes built on it and this is to go ahead despite bitter op-position.

No longer, it seems, is Green Belt land being guarded as it should be. When I was on the local paper in the late 1970s, there were calls to grow Luton Airport and for a housing expansion that would in effect have joined Stevenage and neigh-bouring Hitchin in one huge conurbation, swallow-ing the villages in between. Thankfully, those plans were thwarted. But the fear is that this new development may be the tip of a house-building iceberg.

The selling off of council homes by the Thatcher Government in the 1980s has had a major impact on the town. Just as my mum had to move away from her roots to find somewhere to live, so it is now in Stevenage. Unless youngsters are in a well-paid job, they cannot afford to buy a home in the town. Even then it can be a struggle. More often, new occupants have moved from London and commute the 30 miles south for work.

It was a shock to see a former home of mine, which I bought for £85,000 in the mid-1990s changing hands for more than £420,000 in 2020.

Growing up in Stevenage was a happy experience. It wasn't Utopian; nowhere is. But it wasn't a bad stab at it. It was a clever and forward-looking feat of planning, even if it had a painful birth.

I may have told my parents I was bored during the school holidays - but usually only because it was raining, or my best mates were away on their family jollies. There was always something to do, if not in an Enid Blyton or AA Milne sense.

The parks were a place to run off a lot of adolescent energy and amuse ourselves. If you had a ball and a pile of jumpers, inevitably you'd soon feel like the Pied Piper (which coincidentally was the name of one local pub). Above all, apart from the odd scrape, I felt very safe in Stevenage. The play schemes were fun and safe, unless you were facing the fast bowling of future England cricketer Roland Butcher. I actually held my bat out at arm's length as he ran in at full pelt – the irony being that Roland always saw himself as an off-spinner who could bat.

I certainly wasn't aware of the current scourge, drugs, when I was growing up. They will have been about but I never moved in those circles. But then, as I was so much into sport, I was not even one for the cigarettes, unlike both my brothers. And besides, it would probably have stunted my growth.

Many of those who moved to Stevenage came from areas of London where you felt you could leave your front doors unlocked. It was never like that in Stevenage. For one thing, we had more nickable stuff. We did suffer a break-in once, though. I was about 11 and the back window was broken and a few bits of cash taken - dinner money and insurances, I think. We had the 'excitement' of having to be fingerprinted for elimination purposes. Today you would get no more than a crime number before sticking in an insurance claim. For a short time, I even fancied doing what would now be forensics work.

I always felt a great sense of belonging in Stevenage, and that feeling of home is still there to a degree when I visit. The place has changed so much and yet it hasn't altered much in my mind. After visiting mum one weekend, I took a stroll round Shephalbury Park, where I spent so much of my youth. Some of the landmark trees were gone, the tennis courts were partly overgrown. The putting green was no more - same, too the old pavilion. Only its concrete base remained, partly overgrown.

They can take away physical structures but ghosts from the past still echo around the place; the fun and the people you have not seen for years. And I was incredibly lucky back then that I didn't have to move away when I first got into my chosen career, newspapers.

7 Read All About It

I could never say newspapers ran through my veins. Not until much later, at least. My dad, a baker by trade, changed jobs many times once he left that kind of work behind, and he often did shift work. I liked it best when he was at Nabisco in Welwyn Garden City and he'd bring home packets of Shredded Wheat, Shreddies and other breakfast goodies. But we still missed our warm daily bread, and oven-fresh rolls each morning.

Once dad got a casual extra job, tending to a work colleague's garden in Aston, a village just outside town, for some extra cash. It was frosty the few spring mornings we'd set off to do the work, cycling up this steep hill past what later became Stevenage Golf Club, doing some weeding and planting, then having a lunchtime drink in the Rose & Crown – eye-balled very closely by the vicar and his snooty disciples: the ladies who probably did the flowers and other church errands. Then we'd cycle back home – thankfully it was downhill pretty much all the way.

Mum was working, combining bringing up three lads with keeping house with toiling in the green-grocer's down the hill. I still shiver when I think of her in that shop in the freezing winters. She'd have those gloves with the fingertips cut out but if the gloves were dark blue, you would not be able to tell where the fabric ended and the frostbite began.

There was no door, save in the pull-down shutter and it could be thick snow outside, the best she could do for a warm-up was a few stolen moments in the office, which had a parafin heater. I think she only thawed out properly when she got a job some time later in the cafeteria at British Home Stores.

After finishing my two-year OND in Business Studies, plus RSA qualifications in shorthand and typing, at Stevenage College of Further Education – which has since been rebranded as a university – it was time to go out into the big world. The secretarial side of this was tough – a class with all girls... and me. After a while they forgot I was there and it was eye-opening, especially not having a sister, to listen in to their conversations and some of the plotting that went on.

I knew I might have to move away to find a job in newspapers, though my college careers officer kept telling me I'd be better off thinking of banking or insurance. I had another of those life-changing moments when she arranged a week's work experience for me with an insurance firm in Potters Bar, a 20-minute train ride away.

First morning, uncomfortable in my suit, white shirt and tie, I got on the train but had an uneasy feeling all the way there – and for once it was not from a British Rail sandwich. When we arrived Potters Bar, I got off and changed platforms – and took the first train back. I knew that such a dull 9-5 job could never be for me and doubled down on my dream.

Off went my CV to a few newspapers, not knowing if they even had a vacancy. But I duly got an interview in the next town, Hitchin, home to the head office of the paper that also served Stevenage and Letchworth. The Gazette was a paid-for weekly broadsheet, well respected and widely read in North Herts. I was taken on as a probationer for six months, with the aim I would then sign up as an indentured apprentice for three years. I soon felt at home.

King & Hutchings' offices in Exchange Yard were a V-shaped warren which you may actually have seen in a different guise – as a glass-fronted architects' premises in the ITV drama Doctor Foster, starring Suranne Jones. A number of scenes were also filmed in Hitchin's Market Square, just outside our former offices.

The paper was well staffed by today's norm, with journalists, printers (compositors and readers), as well as advertising and promotions people upstairs.

The Editor, Roy Lomas, was a tall, grey-haired somewhat remote chap who never mixed socially with his troops. He walked with a slight stoop and always seemed to be sucking on a pipe. He had son named Tudor and certainly seemed to be from a distant age himself - though perhaps not that far back.

The Chief Reporter, Bob Folkes, was in the wrong job: he should have been a civil servant. You could set your watch by him, only you didn't need to as he brought his own one in – he had a small travel alarm clock that he'd unfold and place on his desk each morning and tuck it back into his briefcase each night at 5.30. He was a creature of habit - home at lunchtime, never even a quick half with his team.

One evening, with the clock ticking on and Mrs F expecting him back for his tea at the pre-ordained time, we had a tip about a possible murder. Bob donned his jacket and said he was heading home: "We'll pick that up in the morning, on the police calls," he said.

Mr Lomas said of him, somewhat sardonically: "I thought Bob would be with us until he died – I just didn't expect him to die on his first day."

The reporters were in one room, sports desk – John Sellers and Chris Murray – the sub-editors and News Editor Jenny Harris were next door. Jenny was a hard-drinking, committed journalists' union activist; John and Chris were, as you'd expect, sports mad and known for their fondness of a pint or three and always terrific company.

John later worked for the Daily Mirror and then set up his own book publishing company, specialising in pet publications that he still puts out at Crufts each year, while Chris went to the Daily Mail before also running his own corporate publishing operation, Barkers Trident. Some years later, in my freelancing days, I worked for Chris on titles for Prudential, BP, some of the big privatised utilities and sometimes the Met Police's own paper, The Job. That involved plodding down to New Scotland Yard. I soon felt at Holmes there.

Roy Lomas and the very mumsy Doris Steed, his secretary, were a further door along. The boss, evidently always a very busy chap, used to have a man come in to cut his hair as he sat at his desk. It was, it has to be said, not an onerous task for the man with the scissors.

There were three subs, all very different characters: Harvey Woollard, a very religious man who I think was a lay preacher; Terry Knight, a bespectacled kind of Roy Cropper figure, complete with strange array of bags that he always had in tow. Roy Roberts resembled an ageing Terry-Thomas, only without the upper-class lothario bit – though as a pipe-smoker he certainly enjoyed a good shag. He was, I seem to recall, a keen snooker and billiards player and we had a hall just along the road from the office.

We had a team of talented photographers who had licence to be creative. Dick Smith was chief reporter and I learned a great deal going out on jobs with him. I later worked with him on some football coaching books. Word has it that when the paper went under, he 'inherited' the picture library. It would have been a fabulous asset.

Bill Smith was brilliant at football, especially when you consider how poor the stadium floodlights were and how much better even top-of-the range phones are now than the cameras they used back then. Snappers needed dark-room skills, too, to get the best out of their work; no PhotoShop trickery.

Nick Lockett, who has taught photography at university and lives in the Derbyshire Dales, had a thing about stunting up shots for the fun of it. I was often his "model". Once he got me to sit on a park bench, reading a copy of The Times, which was then a broadsheet, while he got a kid on a skateboard to race up to me, leap over my head and jump back on the board, which had carried on its journey between my feet. I wish I'd kept a copy of it. The lad was good. We only had to do it a couple of times – and there were no injuries.

I still remember the first story I wrote. It was from a press release about a church and the beautiful parquet floor they had found underneath some old carpet that had been removed from it. My intro went on about them being "well and truly floored" by the discovery. People who know me will groan and agree it was downhill all the way from there. I should have gone for the mat finish.

There was the inevitable round of council meetings, courts and village fetes. At one, a pumpkin show in Pirton, I met a girl, Gillian, and we dated for a time. Yes, my first serious girlfriend. Her parents ran one of the village pubs (I missed out there...). Gillian has long since made the sensible choice of life partner and lives near Cambridge and it is good that we are still in occasional touch today.

Our usual haunts were the Chinese restaurant and the Regal cinema in Hitchin, as well as the town's fine selection of hostelries, before her mum drove to collect her.

Thursdays were our slack day as the paper had just hit the streets. Lunch would stray well beyond the allotted hour and would always be spent in a pub – there were so many to choose from but we tended to stick to the KA (King's Arms) where darts were a frequent cause of tension, and later the Red Hart, which we called "the Red Ant" after it was briefly closed following "an insect hygiene issue".

There were no set initiation rites for newbie reporters, such as some I have heard of – none of the apocryphal getting the junior to phone "Mr C Lion" at the zoo, or "Mr Clapp" at the Special Clinic.

But my first Thursday drinkies saw me down three pints of Abbot Ale and wobble back to the office, whereupon I accidentally kicked over the bright red metal fire bucket, filled with water, and flooded the painted stone corridor that ran the length of the building.

The editor then wandered in, or I should say almost waded in, and gave me a knowing sideways look as I sat in a haze at my desk, before quietly organising a clean-up. Nothing was said. He didn't need to. I was mortified. Pissed but mortified.

Stevenage office, where I was later based, had a feature writer, Martha Snowdon, who was snapper Bill Smith's partner; a brilliantly laid-back chief reporter, Barrie Dack; his deputy Barbara, who later married Chris Murray, plus a handful of us scribes. So many from the paper went on to bigger things: David Foster was a Sky News and al-Jazeera anchor man, several others such as Hugh Bateson worked on the Mail, the Independent or, like Clive Hutchby, edited regional dailies. Tim Collings set up his own sports news agency and wrote several Formula 1 books. He would get the waiter at his local Italian restaurant to translate the Italian sports papers for him and sell on any half-decent stories to his Fleet Street contacts.

Clive worked in the Letchworth office and we used to have telephone chess games when I was based in Hitchin. They would last days – he'd usually win. He now lives in the Lake District and has produced some fabulous re-workings and plottings of the famed Alfred Wainwright walk books.

Kit Galer taught me page design by not teaching it to me – he merely pointed out all the cardinal sins to avoid then left me to it. He had taken over from John Sellers as sports editor and would hold court in the pub. He was immensely funny. John's humour was drier and his match reports were always entertaining reading. with a very easy style that made you feel you were at the game.

Kit was always looking for an outlet for his mirth and wrote sketches for TV, notably for the Two Ronnies, including one you can find on YouTube of two London Underground workers who get on a train and weave the names of dozens of Tube stations into their conversation, such as: "Mornington Crescent, Harrow-on-the-Hill are you?". I believe he still gets the occasional small royalty cheque when it is repeated around the world.

He now lives in Melbourne, Australia, where he took Rupert Murdoch's dollar for many years, and his periodic returns to the old country in search of a proper drop of warm beer and to do a roll-call of old colleagues always inspire a Gazette reunion. Those lunch times were worth going to work for. Laugh? I thought my legs would never dry.

The office in Stevenage Old Town was a timbered building, which is still there, with wobbly, creaking floors and ill-fitting doors, located immediately above a newsagents. We even had a manned front desk – few if any exist today – which was a useful source of stories from people dropping in while they were shopping. We also had a new midweek free paper, a tabloid, to keep us busy.

I remember the first time I had a picture byline on a front page story. A young lad had shinned up a pylon and relieved himself on a high-voltage line above the main London railway. I went to the inquest and had to interview the parents and try to get a photo. It is still one of my proudest memories to have received a note from the parents thanking me for the empathetic way I reported the story. They understood that I was just doing a job and were way more forgiving of my intrusion than I might have been had I been in their shoes.

As part of my training, I had two, eight-week block release courses at Harlow College. The NCTJ proficiency test would be key to my progress. Chatting one day to Stevenage chief reporter Barrie Dack – a brilliant boss who would put you right in the kindest way – I learned how I had come to be taken on.

It had been my cunning plan to do shorthand and typing at college that had paid off. "Everyone who applied could at least match your qualifications," said Barrie, "and some had more. But you were the only one we could send out on a job from Day One. You could take a reliable note and type a story up. It showed that you were determined and had thought ahead about things."

Barrie pushed my need for accuracy by giving me six months of covering court – Stevenage magistrates, on Mondays, Hitchin magistrates the next day, Stevenage again on Thursdays, and Hitchin, for inquests, on Fridays. Occasionally I'd get the full set, with Letchworth magistrates on a Thursday.

I quite enjoyed it and would always come back with a full notebook. You got to know the ushers and solicitors, who would tip you off if anything good was coming up. One time we had Lester Piggott, the famous jockey, in court on a speeding charge. He'd been on his way between race meetings, chasing winners. The fine would have been small beer to him but the ban was more taxing for him. Which is ironic given that, in 1987, the former champion jockey was jailed at Ipswich Crown Court for three years after being found guilty of a £3.2m tax fraud.

The nine-times Derby winner, who had a personal fortune estimated at more than £20m, is said to have used different names to channel his earnings into secret bank accounts in Switzerland, the Bahamas, Singapore and the Caymans. He was stripped of his OBE, which is rather more harsh treatment than for some who game the system today.

Inquests could often test my ability to keep a straight face at some of the tragi-comic ways that people had met their maker. One, for a man who plunged 10 storeys at his workplace, had me in secret agony – Python fans will know the "Biggus Dickus" scene well. When the police constable said the poor chap had been "very popular at work and everybody knew him from the top floor downwards", I had visions of him saying goodbye to them all on the way down to a messy clocking out.

These were the days before fax machines or electronic connectivity and we used to send our typed words to head office in an envelope which we handed to the driver of the most convenient Hitchin-bound bus. You then rang the Hitchin office to say the parcel was on a certain timed bus and someone would be dispatched to collect it.

But it was not unknown for the person who took the message to get distracted and forget to go – and the envelope would end up either in the depot or back on its way to Stevenage, where we would re-trieve it and try again. On a press day, Barrie would drive the last bits over, to make sure they got there on time - or, indeed, at all.

I started doing some sports reporting at weekends and it was a fun leveller to write about players per-forming for their senior clubs – Stevenage, Hitchin or Letchworth – on a Saturday then have them kick me up in the air on a Sunday morning.

My team, from the league's third tier, was drawn one year against the all-conquering Twin Foxes, who had been National Sunday Cup finalists twice in three years. I went to their player of the year awards on the Friday night before our tie and cock-ily warned them how we would be up for a giant-killing that weekend.

In the first five minutes, I went round their goal-keeper, to be faced with an open goal and shot from the edge of the box – only for a defender, Terry Rowney, to come from nowhere and make a ridicu-lous, full-stretch clearance on the line. We lost 16-0 and got very good at taking kick-offs. Poor Dave Pickard in our goal must have had backache. The follow-up banter was decent, though.

There were some enjoyable sporting moments, especially in cricket. The Herts county representative team of club players were paired one year with a senior Essex side packed with international Test players. A new reporter, Harry Walton, a graduate whose dad was editor of the Swindon Advertiser, was despatched to phone across updates at regular intervals as it was press day.

Herts made hard work of their 153 all out at Hitchin's ground and we felt sure Essex would knock the runs off in very short order. They were coasting at 71-2 with England batsman Graham Gooch newly in, but every time poor H trekked to the phone box outside the ground to call in with his words, he'd miss a clutch of Essex wickets tumbling. Hertfordshire skittled them out for just 120, with four wickets going to a little-known spinner, Dilip Doshi, who went on to play Test cricket for India.

The biggest event on our patch by a mile was the Knebworth music festival. In 1975, some 100,000 fans packed the stately home's grounds just outside Stevenage to see Pink Floyd, the Steve Miller Band and Captain Beefheart. But the big one form those days that I recall was the following year, when the Rolling Stones,10cc and Lynyrd Skynyrd were on the bill. It was billed th Hot August night. And it was.

Somewhere between 150,000 and 200,000 attended and for the £4.50 ticket price they got the added bonus of a streaker. He clambered onto the stage, then leapt off, breaking both ankles. That's naked ambition for you. "Hey, you, get off of my stage..."

The show overran. It was supposed to finish by midnight but, after the Stones' set, which began with Satisfaction – of which there was clearly plenty – finished about 2am, David (Lord) Cobbold, the owner of Knebworth House, was fined £2,000 for the licence breach. It must have been worth it to see Mick Jagger in black leather and tights – an outfit that one paper described as making him look "like a gay Richard III".

One of our reporters got an incredible pre-show exclusive. He found out where the Stones were staying and rang the hotel, never expecting to be put through. Mick Jagger picked up the phone and chatted for ages about the gig and the band. The Gazette printed thousands of extra copies and ran supplements before the event, with papers being sold at the train and bus stations as well as outside the Knebworth Park venue.

Afterwards, the paper was packed with photos and stories of the inevitable aftermath – the litter mountains and the odd person still too drunk, or stoned, to realise it was all over.

I didn't see the Stones' show but I did go when the Beach Boys played there in 1980. I'd really gone for Mike Oldfield and it was a kind of home show for Elkie Brooks, whose husband, a sound engineer, came from Stevenage and they got maried just up the road from our office.

Knebworth was a fixture for many years and the likes of Oasis, Cliff Richard, Robbie Williams, Status Quo, Oink Floyd, Dire Straits, Elton John, Eric

Clapton and Phil Collins with Genesis have brought many hundreds of thousands to the area to see them. I think Robbie had three sell-out shows or 125,000 there in 2003 but since then th event has been somewhat scaled back. So much so, Chas and Dave were among the performers at the last Knebworth festival, in 2014.

Halcyon days. For me, though, not long into my journalistic career in 1976, there was lots more sport to cover.

8 Earning my stripes

I can't remember the first football match I went to, and that is both a surprise and disappointment. Isn't it supposed to be like your first day at school, your first wedding or the birth of your first child? I strongly suspect it was a Southern League Division One game: Stevenage Town v Tunbridge Wells Rangers on August 22, 1966.

A yellowing programme from the following home game that season tells me that 1,657 souls, likely including my 10-year-old self, had witnessed that earlier match, a 6-0 victory for the Stripes, with three goals each for the lightning-paced Robin

Chandler and the gangly but effective Peter Walker, known to fans as "Annie Walker," after the sour-faced landlady of Coronation Street's Rovers Return. That result apparently lured me back to Broadhall Way a few days later, when the Stripes – they played in red and white, with red shorts – beat Trowbridge Town 1-0.

By contrast, my first visit to Tottenham Hotspur a couple of years later, with near-neighbour Paul Cork and his dad George for an FA Cup Fifth-round tie against Liverpool, made a far more indelible impression. Especially as my big hero, Jimmy Greaves, scored for Spurs in a 1-1 draw.

I wonder if the reason I don't recall those early Stevenage games is because I didn't share them with my dad, who was not interested in the game, or any of the mates I kicked about with. Nonetheless, I do remember being so close to the touchline that I could smell the embrocation on the players' legs and feel the thuds of the studs when some especially spicy challenges flew about. Southern League Division One was not for the faint-hearted.

Some of the players looked so tough that you suspected they might one day feature in a news report ending with the words "the trial continues". But there was some "working men's ballet" to be seen, too. I'd watch Dickie England or Colin 'Paddy' Powell storming down the touchline at full pace and want to be a winger. They had thighs like tugboats and lungs the size barrage balloons. I had a long way to go...

Town were the club two iterations before the current one, which was rebranded from Stevenage Borough FC to Stevenage FC in 2010. But a look back through the history of football in Stevenage reveals clubs with the names Wednesday, United, Youth, Rovers, Corinthians, Red Cross – and even, for the season 1898-99, Stevenage New Town Rovers. Odd, that last one, because Stevenage did not become a designated New Town until 1946.

Town had competed in the Spartan, Delphian, Luton and District and the North Herts leagues. They and the club's successor, Stevenage Athletic, both went bust – the latter having had something of a grave quite literally dug for it by its owner, a Maltese businessman of doubtful provenance.

There were two stands at what is now known as the Lamex Stadium when I first started going: a decent-sized brick one and a rickety wooden-slatted one at the Broadhall Way end that always seemed a potential death trap. Fans did their best to test my theory each week with their foot-stamping antics. I swear I saw it sway all the while.

One strong memory is of The Beatles' Penny Lane being played at each match, although that was not released until early 1967. Another hit single I recall being spun relentlessly like a hapless full-back by a classy winger was The Supremes' You Can't Hurry Love, which was a hit in the latter half of 1966.

Today, a shiny new North Stand – paid for largely through a supporters' debenture scheme, gives the club an enhanced roadside appeal and a much more professional air, for all their struggles in the lower reaches of the Football League, exacerbated by the coronavirus pandemic in 2020, when the club's tireless community work won great plaudits.

It now has a modern stadium with seating at both ends and along one side, and a home terraced East Stand – though that was designed so that seating could be installed without need for a rebuild.

Prior to that, in the club's Vauxhall Conference days, it was more ramshackle, and I watched a famous 4-0 Easter Monday thrashing of Woking in 1996 that all but secured Borough the league title – though not promotion – from that East Terrace side of the ground, balanced precariously on a pile of plastic bread crates for a better view amid a full house and a delayed kick-off.

There was always something appealing in earlier days when the crowd changed ends at half-time to stand behind the goal your team was attacking. And it was never so sparse that they announced the crowd changes to the team.

After such a chequered history, it is astonishing to recall how, in 2012, Stevenage were in the League One play-offs, battling for a place in the second-tier Championship, before losing to Sheffield United, latterly of the Premier League, giddy heights for a club with low average gates but, at that time, a team at whose core was a tight-knit group of talented players who had enjoyed two promotions, from the Conference, and then from League Two via the play-offs. Earlier the club enjoyed the distinction of winning the first competitive cup final at the new Wembley Stadium, the FA Trophy in 2007 – a game I missed with the lame excuse that I was living and working in New Zealand at the time.

Crowds at Town games varied wildly between a hardy couple of hundred and just over 1,000, affected by whether Tottenham or Arsenal were playing at home, which they invariably were on alternate weekends.

My preferred station from which to watch the action when I was new to secondary school was the 'bread crate terrace', up against the metal railing. I had very few there for company and a great view, right along the edge of the penalty box. Occasionally I'd have to shimmy along if a linesman got in my way.

It was the season after England's World Cup win and football was gripped by a wave of optimism and renewed interest. The ground was a 15- to 20-minute walk from my home, past my old junior school, Roebuck.

That stroll, even when I have made it in recent times, still brings a sense of pre-match excitement. And there was always something almost spiritual about a foggy Monday night at Stevenage under the floodlights.

Town finished third in the Southern League First Division in that 1966-67 season, behind Dover and Margate, and were promoted to the Premier Division. They had powerful ball-winners alongside the former Spurs and England midfielder Johnny

Brooks, who pulled the strings. There was the barrel-chested, no-nonsense centre-half John Mills, and a very tidy goalkeeper, Ray Peacock. Peter Walker and Roy Cutler carved up the goals between them.

Sadly, that success was to be short-lived: the club was wound up after finishing 18th out of 22 the following season. You could see the financial travails of the club even in the production of its match programmes, which degenerated to penny team-sheets.

This team showed its capabilities, though, on a memorable evening in February 1967. It was a special encounter against Fourth Division Port Vale for England legend Sir Stanley Matthews, who was then aged 52 and on his farewell tour. It was a school night, so I was not allowed to go, but a jam-packed Broadhall Way was treated to a 4-3 home win, with Brooks putting on a masterclass – outshining even Sir Stan, who played professionally into his fifties. With the ground full, fans desperate to see the game resorted to shinning up trees and even the floodlight pylons for a glimpse of the old maestro.

Town's final competitive match was a 1-1 draw at Hillingdon Borough. Out of the club's embers rose Stevenage Athletic, competing in the Metropolitan League. The team sheet was unrecognisable from the old Town team and they were without a ground for the first eight games of the season before moving in to Broadhall Way with a new manager, Jim Briscoe. Jim was a remarkable character, enormously likeable but known for the odd fit of temper and, shall we say, an innocent lack of self-awareness.

Kit Galer tells a couple of famous tales about Jim – who was known at Broadhall Way as "Mr Stevenage" for his five decades-long association with the club, from manager to groundsman.

Jim's playing career as a centre-forward in League football was cut short by war. His debut for Sheffield Wednesday came in a wartime derby with Sheffield United in 1943 – but he had the distinction of playing in front of an incredible 132,000 crowd in Amsterdam for the Combined Services' match against Holland in the first post-War "international".

He was a prolific goalscorer – three in five games for Wednesday after the war, only to find himself in the reserves; a 55-goal record season in the Kent League with Ramsgate, and nine in four games for Gainsborough Trinity. He was lured to Stevenage in 1967 as commercial manager by team boss Tommy Bickerstaff, who then promptly upped sticks for Cambridge United. When the club folded shortly afterwards, Jim, having moved his family from Kent, stayed and his legend began.

Kit recalls an occasion recounted by Jim's assistant at the time, Brian Parker. At half-time in one away game, Jim was fuming, his face glowing like a roaring beacon, after his team's embarrassing display. He steamed into the dressing room and began throwing filled teacups around – only to be reminded that he had gone into the opposing team's dressing room.

Another time, Jim "invented" a whole new playing

formation: 4-4-3. After explaining it in elaborate detail to his players, who had sat in bemused silence, the goalkeeper, who apparently had not been factored into Jim's cunning plan, put his hand up and opined: "Er, boss... what about me?" It was a famous facepalm moment – and you have to wonder how the rest of the team talk went.

But Kit's favourite Briscoe story was the aftermath of a shock Herts Senior Cup defeat at the hands of South Midlands League Baldock. Jim stormed into the dressing room to give his shamefaced players a right dressing down. The Baldock stadium had a communal bath and a plate of sandwiches for the players was sitting on the side. "Well, you're not fookin' having them," said Jim, sweeping the plate and sarnies into the filled bath.

"It's all right, Jim," said captain Alan Barker, "we've had ours. Those are Baldock's."

Jim was larger than life, and I would often see him at the ground when I was programme editor for a spell in the mid-1990s. He'd always offer a cheery wave when he was busy mowing the pitch or touching up some paintwork. His abiding mission from the day he arrived was to see Stevenage play in the Football League.

Current chairman Phil Wallace, who has led the club more than 20 years, speaking after Jim died in 2014, with Boro having achieved that mission, said: "Jim was a guide and inspiration to me when I joined the club. His dream to get the club into the League drove me on. He was the first person I thought of when the whistle blew against Kidderminster and we had done it."

Jim and his wife Mary were there during times good and bad and were like family to a succession of players they took in at lodgers over the years. On the field, after taking over as manager, Jim got the club back to the heights of the old Town club, in the Southern League. And he gave me my first big scoop as a junior reporter.

I had been walking home past the ground one evening when I noticed the lights were on in the Boardroom. Former Spurs and Scotland striker Alan Gilzean was team manager at this time, with Jim his assistant. The door was ajar and I knocked. Jim was there, with a couple of the directors. He was on the phone but he invited me in while carrying on his call. "This will interest you, son," he said.

"I've got Gilly on the phone and we have been talking about getting Jimmy Greaves up here to play. If it comes off, Gilly will come out of retirement, too, and they will team up as they used to for Spurs. How about that?!"

I was stunned – two of my biggest heroes playing for Stevenage? "Here," he said, passing the phone to me. Gilzean, a gruff Scot, duly repeated what Jim had said and I knew I had a story that would feature on our back and front pages next week – and be picked up by the nationals.

It was a Friday evening and I spent that weekend sweating on whether the news would get out before I could break it in the Gazette the following Thursday. Jim promised me I'd have the tale to myself. He was true to his word.

I didn't have a phone number for John Sellers, the Sports Editor, so I dashed off some handwritten notes at home and took them in to John first thing on Monday. John's main role was to cover Stevenage matches and even he hadn't had wind of this amazing turn of events. Naturally he had to check it out with his contacts at the club and not just take the word of a rather overexcited junior reporter.

He made his calls while I hammered away at the old black Triumph Imperial typewriter, bashing out my words. John tidied them before they went into print and did a write-off for the front page.

"That's brilliant, our kid. You can stay!" John said. "It's kosher. We might even have to put your name on this one... and there is a pint of Abbot with your name on it at lunchtime." I kept it to just the one.

The 'G-men' plan had been a last-ditch, desperate revenue-raising bid for a club in deep trouble financially. And while it never actually came off, it was still a brilliant exclusive tale, all factually correct when I wrote it. It certainly raised my profile locally, for a time at least.

That summer, Stevenage Athletic went the way of Town, only with more long-lasting damaging effects in terms of lost trust and goodwill, especially with commercial supporters. However, Jim Briscoe's dream, if we did but know it then, was not dead, it was merely pining.

The postscript to my big story came some years

later when I learned that Greaves had been in no state to make any kind of comeback in 1976. He had been in a clinic to deal with his chronic alcoholism. A further twist came when I mentioned it to Jimmy himself in early 1998 when he visited the club.

Stevenage Borough had been drawn to play Newcastle United in the FA Cup Fourth Round and The Sun was sponsoring the game, which went out live on Sky TV. Jimmy, as a Sun columnist, came to chat to Boro manager Paul Fairclough, who invited me along because a chat with Jimmy would make a great spread for the match programme, which I was putting together.

At the end, I asked Jimmy – who beat his drink problems and won his wife Irene back – if he recalled the day he might have signed for Stevenage. He couldn't at all. I told him what had happened, and he said he'd had no idea about the plan but would have gone along with it for his big pal Gilly, had he been able to. It was a real treat to spend an hour or so with the biggest football hero of my boyhood.

Gilzean became a reclusive character. He dropped off the radar. James Morgan's 2010 book, In Search of Alan Gilzean, was a tale of a country-wide hunt that bore no fruit. Greaves said Gilzean was the greatest he played with. But they hadn't set eyes on each other "for the best part of 40 years" when they finally caught up with each other again in Guernsey, at a Spurs legends evening.

"We hugged," recalls Gilzean. "He said: 'where have

you been?' I said: 'Keeping away from you!'." By then Greaves was confined to a wheelchair but it was Gilzean, one of the most intelligent players Scotland has produced and a master header of the ball, who fell ill suddenly and died in July 2018, aged 79. He had a brain tumour. Jimmy was heartbroken.

Stevenage Athletic's demise was not a surprise. But it was acrimonious because of club owner Javier Revuelta's objection to a phoenix club, assembled by Keith Berners and team manager Vic Folbigg, wanting to use the ground, which was owned by Stevenage Development Corporation but leased to Athletic.

Revuelta, I discovered from a trip to Companies House in London, had a less than unblemished business record, with at least one bankruptcy filed against his name, and claimed he had a 38-year lease on the ground. He wanted to use it for a market and any other commercial role he could put it to, such as car parking for Knebworth music festivals. But the lease permitted football as its sole purpose and the Development Corporation called on Revuelta to forfeit the lease.

A stand-off ensued. Stevenage FC had arranged a match against Hitchin Youth at the stadium. Revuelta was having none of it. One morning he had a JCB plough a deep trench through the pitch, wrecking the surface and the drainage beneath, rendering it unplayable. Football would not return there for some years. Instead, the council allowed the new club use of a roped-off pitch at the King

George V playing fields beside the town centre.

There were always problems with the pitch at Broadhall Way. Players often had to be helped off with blood pouring from gashed knees as stones and flints found their way to the surface. Kit once persuaded Jim Briscoe to let a photographer snap some shots of players seemingly digging up potatoes from the edge of the penalty area.

Athletic had some very good players but too few to climb the heights they thought they should have scaled. Midfielder Paul Peterson was a graduate of the Leeds United "academy" and a contemporary of Norman Hunter and Terry Yorath, both of whom turned out for a special "all-star" game in 1980 when Broadhall Way was finally back in harness. I put together the programme for that milestone match.

Jose Whishaw was another talented midfielder, with a good tactical understanding and a demeanour which I thought would lead him into club management, as Peterson had done when he was assistant to Paul Fairclough. But if Jose was not to be a leading light, his son Ben very much was – you may know him as an actor in the Bond films, as the nerdy gadget guy, Q, among many other brilliant roles in movies and in TV dramas.

A new chapter had begun for Stevenage football – and for me as, by then, I had moved on from the local paper, first to West London, then, after a brief return to North Herts as Gazette Sports editor, to Fleet Street: The Sporting Life and then the new

Mail on Sunday, which launched in May 1982 at the start of the Falklands war.

In the mid-1990s, I'd be back with Boro, as programme editor during one of their most infamous sagas – the FA Cup clashes with Newcastle United, of which more later. But I was out of the mix when the club finally achieved Football League status after a long and fraught road in 2010.

I did though get to see them at the zenith - a play-off with Sheffield United for a place in the Championship. Boro lost and have since been relegated and struggled in the lower reaches of League Two for a time.

They have, however, consistently proved their value as a community club, providing meals for the elderly and vulnerable during the Covid lockdown and all manner of other initiatives. It is no wonder they seem to win League community club awards each year. They do the town proud.

But, back in the day, for Boro – for a short time at least –at least, the only way was up...

9 Lords of the Rings

One of the things your sports editor doesn't tell you when you are a young reporter sent to cover boxing for the first time is that, sitting in your ringside seat, you might get the odd splatter of blood on your notebook. Or your tie.

Being up close and personal – more so than with most other sports – brings home the utter brutality of the ring. You can, however, get too close to the action, as a photographer colleague on another of my former papers did when he went to get some snaps of polo, at the Guards Club, near Windsor. Dave Crump, having not covered polo before, decided it was probably just like covering football, so he stationed himself and all his kit behind one goal. He was there, on his fold-up canvas seat, camera raised – but soon beat a panicked retreat when he saw a number of fast-galloping, heavy horses filling his viewfinder and the riders flailing mallets high above their heads. Colleagues used to wind him after that, offering him a Polo mint.

Viewed through whatever lens you choose, boxing is real and people get hurt – and not in cartoon fashion. Watching from so close, it also becomes evident why you have judges sitting on different sides of the ring. All too often you'll have a debate in the bar afterwards and say to someone: "Have we even seen the same fight?"

Nonetheless, it was a thrill to have covered a number of major noble sporting battles, from world title fights to amateur club bouts.

And while the sport is indisputably violent, there is a special code that goes with the discipline of the ring and boxing has been the welcome salvation of many a young boy with a troubled background or chaotic home life. You should not judge a book by its cover, so it is with boxers. They may have disfigured faces and appear as hard as nails but they can be some of the nicest, gentle-natured sportsmen you'll meet – at least when they take off their game face. I saw it first hand.

A towering figure in Stevenage when I was a young reporter was Geoff Glencross, whose dad Stanley was a founder member of the local amateur boxing club and got Geoff involved at the age of eight. He ended up having more than 70 bouts, winning five national titles.

Having quit the ring, Geoff moved on to training and mentoring successive generations, turning out not just decent boxers but good young men. A club fight night was always great entertainment and they would rustle up a big boxing name to hand out the prizes. That way I got to meet the likes of Maurice Hope, Alan Minter, Terry Marsh and Lloyd Honeyghan and to chat about their exploits.

Working for a local paper, I would be hot on any boxers making a name for themselves nationally – or internationally. Placid Gonzales was the first. What a name for a boxer! Actually, it was a family thing – that moniker was given to the first-born son. Placid tore up all those 'punch-drunk' boxer memes by going on to be a financial advisor with a succession of blue-chip firms. If you wanted to be hit with some life cover or a personal pension, he was yer man. He could even get you a current account with the Queen's bank, Coutts.

Plass was fiercely competitive, naturally, and that came out not only in the ring but on the snooker table, too. I always told him he only beat me because he had reach advantage... but he knew his way round the green baize as well as a 20-foot square ring and was always great company, with a range of opinions on so many things and they didn't always match my own, so there was some interesting sparring, too.

In May 1977, as a light-heavyweight representing Hitchin Youth, Placid battled his way to the ABA Finals at Wembley Arena – amateur boxing's biggest night of the year, which went out on TV. Unfortunately, he found Welshman Chris Lawson a shade too good that evening.

That was a quality finals, though, with Charlie Magri (flyweight), Pat Cowdell (bantam) and Colin Jones (welterweight), going on to become big names in the paid ranks, all winning on that bill. A year later, Placid's return journey to Wembley was halted when he lost in the Home Counties qualifying rounds.

But the good folk of Hitchin and North Herts were not without a pugilistic star for long. Andy Straughn, who also fought out of Placid's club and was trained by Harry Goodwin, did even better. He won three successive ABA titles at light-heavyweight - one more even than the great Sir Henry Cooper – and competed for Great Britain at the 1980 Moscow Olympics.

Born on Christmas Day (clearly one day early!) in Barbados in 1959, Andy moved to England with his family when he was 10. Just nine years later he was an Olympian, competing for his adopted homeland. He recalls: "All my boxing tuition came from here, so competing for Great Britain was a no-brainer."

Andy is very unassuming out of the ring and certainly didn't become arrogant after that early success. "At the time, I didn't appreciate what I'd achieved and how big it was," he said. "But it changed my life. I was young – but when I came back from Moscow, I grew up. My coaches clearly saw something that I didn't know I had in me."

I saw Andy's ABA title wins; he owned that Wembley ring, it seemed. In May 1979, he beat Welshman Aneurin Williams, of the Semtex club in Brynmawr. Nothing too explosive about him... the club was attached to the Dunlop Semtex rubber factory.

As a measure of how Andy was shaping up, two future British champions, Terry Marsh and Jim McDonnell, were beaten finalists that evening. They were ring royalty.

"I can remember everything about it," says Andy. "The noise, the dressing room – and being on TV for the first time. I was still very young and hadn't expected to get to the finals at all. It was a kind of 'let's give it a go and see how far I get' thing. But it didn't worry me at all."

Twelve months later, as hot favourite, Andy was back, accompanied by three coachloads of fans, including his parents and five siblings, to outpoint his England camp sparring partner Devon Bailey, of Battersea. It was a performance that took the eye of the GB selectors, with the Moscow Olympics on the horizon.

Next in the ring that evening was a massively-hyped teenager from Wandsworth named Frank Bruno. He had a huge, noisy following and cut an imposing figure as he hauled himself between the ropes just above my head. It was the final bout on the card and, much as I wanted to get some reaction from Andy back in the dressing room, I just had to see what all the fuss was about, amid the deafening roars of "Bruno!... Bruno!".

At just 18, Frank beat Welshman Rudy Pika easily on points to become the youngest ABA champion in history. His movements looked stiff, his gait almost musclebound, but the power that would take him to the brink of the world heavyweight title was there for all to see. Yet Bruno didn't go to Moscow: Andy Straughn did.

Frank turned pro and formed his famed double act with BBC commentator Harry Carpenter. "You know what I mean, Harreee?" A panto star in the making, for sure. For Andy, Moscow was no pantomime but it was theatre.

For a time, though, even getting there wasn't a certainty. The US was boycotting the Games in protest at the Soviet invasion of Afghanistan and put pressure on Britain to do the same. US President Jimmy Carter proposed, to end the impasse, that the event should move permanently to a site in Greece, their spiritual home, but the International Olympics Committee (IOC) shot that idea down. Carter was trying to head off a reciprocal boycott for 1984, in Atlanta. His plan failed. China and others, particularly Kenya, whose long-distance runners were missed, sat out Moscow, while teams and individuals from some nations, such as New Zealand, competed under the Olympic flag as their Government had supported the boycott but did not enforce it.

So Andy, at just 19, flew to Moscow to represent

Britain; he had all the kit and a big dreams as he packed his bags for the Russian capital. He remembers being at the Opening Ceremony with his teammates and then in the athletes' village, sharing an accommodation block with the likes of Daley Thompson and Sharron Davies. Daley won gold in the decathlon, swimmer Sharron a silver but was cheated of gold by Petra Schneider, of East Germany, who used performance-enhancing drugs.

"We were given stacks of all sorts of kit and mementoes by the sponsors and organisers," says Andy. "I think most of my family got trainers and tops! I had to pinch myself at times in the village, seeing all these faces I knew from the papers and TV. I wondered what I was doing there. It was a release when I got to training, to make me realise why."

It was his ill fortune to get a tough draw in the round of 16, though, and he was beaten by the raucously-backed home favourite, David Kvachadze, a Georgian representing the Soviet Union. The referee stopped it in the second of three rounds. "He was tough but I played into his hands by trying to make a fight of it," says Andy. "I should have boxed him instead of going to war, letting him pick me off. But he was 28, a grown man, and I was still young, with so much to learn. It fired me up to get better."

Kvachadze didn't feature in the medals. Andy returned to Hitchin with his stock still high and his longer-term plans undented. He had the hat-trick of ABA titles to complete – and did so, beating Dennis Bailey the following May. "After that," he recalls, "there was talk of turning pro, though Harry Goodwin didn't want me to. He was worried about me being managed by 'gangsters', as he put it."

Terry Greenaway, another well-respected boxing coach in North Herts, was more supportive, saying that Andy had nothing more to prove in the amateur ranks. Andy recalls: "I was impressed with manager Burt McCarthy's offer. He said he would put me on a wage of £150 a week and I could keep all the purse money I won. He wouldn't take a penny from me until I won a British title – and he was true to his word. He is in his 90s now and still keeps in touch."

McCarthy was a wealthy businessman with jewellery interests in London's Hatton Garden. Andy often worked for him at jewellery parties, handing round items for inspection – and that is how he met wife, Debs. "I had the jewels, but I met a gem!" We've now been married 30 years," he says, probably within his wife's earshot.

Andy made the step into the professional game in 1982 and won seven of his first eight fights, the other a draw, before heading to Detroit with his new stablemate and soon-to-be close friend – indeed almost a brother – Errol Christie, as guests of the famed Kronk gym, run by trainer Emanuel Steward. The boys would become inseparable. McCarthy believed the US trip would progress their boxing education. The Kronk gym was a champion-making factory and one of the first people they met was Thomas 'Hitman' Hearns. Errol sparred with Hearns and impressed the American, earning his instant respect.

But in Detroit, the murder capital of the Mid-West if not the US, they found a mix of horror and wonderment. The place brought to life in Eminem's 8-Mile was somewhere you had to stay forever on your guard, with "pill-heads and alcoholics everywhere".

One day, while they were at a hairdressers, Andy and Errol witnessed a woman being carjacked at gunpoint outside. She was shaken less by the event, it seems, than the lads, who rushed to her aid. They had seen crime in east London but nothing as stark as this. The victim brushed it off as almost matter of fact, which shocked them.

Andy was convinced the Americans at the gym thought the pair were just "two plucky Brits who deserved nothing more than to be flattened for daring even to walk into the Kronk".

There were a couple of bouts for Andy while they were in Detroit and he lost them both, but it was felt to have been a valuable part of his boxing journey. Back in the UK, though, the pair were hopelessly in debt. While in the States, they'd still had to keep paying rent and bills on their flat in Brockley, east London. Errol, who died in June 2017 from lung cancer aged 53, was quoted in his book, "No Place to Hide", as saying: "We came back as world-class boxers but with little or nothing in our pockets."

For Christie, a big-money fight with West Ham's Mark Kaylor would do much for his bank balance. Andy was not in that money-earning league but at least went unbeaten in his next eight contests, seven of them wins. He would go on to lift the British cruiserweight title twice – each time beating the same opponent, Tee Jay, from Clapham.

The first clash against Taju Akay, to give him his formal name, was in October 1986 for the title vacated by Sammy Reeson. Andy's handy opponent had fought for Ghana at the 1984 Olympics in Atlanta and won, then lost, the British cruiserweight crown. Cheered on by a noisy "home" crowd in North Herts, at Stevenage Leisure Centre, Andy won, to claim the Lonsdale Belt, by 117-and-a-half points to 117.

It was a brilliant night and I recall McCarthy talking up the broader horizons of his young charge. But Andy's reign would last only until February and his first defence, when he was outpointed by Roy Smith, of Nottingham, at Alfreton – a bout watched by Brian Clough, who was then the Nottingham Forest manager.

That came as a big blow but Andy was determined to regain the crown. "I won the belt then went on holiday to Barbados. When I came back, I didn't give myself enough time to get fully fit. I was only a little bit off – but I should never have lost to him," he said.

Next up was a title eliminator against Glenn McCrory in Oldham. It was a close 10-rounder, with Durham-born McCrory, who had stepped down from heavyweight, won by TKO in the last round. McCrory, now a TV and radio pundit, went on to win British, Commonwealth and IBF world titles before losing to Lennox Lewis for the British and European heavyweight belts. Straughn, meanwhile, would win three and lose three of his final six bouts.

In 1988, he regained the British crown, outpointing Tee Jay, this time in Reading. There was something of an admission afterwards, though, when he said: "It feels great, but a year earlier the belt would not have fitted me as I was about two stone overweight."

This was in November and he didn't fight again until the following May, defending against Johnny Nelson in the 'Super Tent' at London's Finsbury Park on the night Michael Watson beat Nigel Benn in a highly-anticipated TV showdown for the Commonwealth middleweight title.

There is a brilliant picture of Andy landing a shot to Nelson's face; sweat flying and glistening in the ring lighting. It showed he had the power to be in and around the best in the division. Nelson had a patchy record and was not fancied but he stopped Andy in eight. That victory lit the touch-paper for Nelson, who became a long-reigning WBO champion.

Andy had one more successful night at Stevenage, delighting his fans by beating Abner Blackstock on points in October 1989, but two successive defeats, to David Muhammed and then Derek Angol – for the Commonwealth title – brought the curtain down on his pro career in March 1990 at the Royal Albert Hall.

Andy had given his family and many fans some

great moments to remember. My youngest brother Kevin recalls one. Kev, who was 17 and has long since lived in the US mid-West, working latterly as a Sheriff's deputy, wanted to come to a fight, so I blagged him a press ticket as a photographer when Andy and Errol were in action in Coventry Leisure Centre in 1983.

Kevin still recalls leaning through the ropes with a camera one of the Gazette's snappers loaned us. "I remember one of the photographers there giving me tips on taking pics, then getting showered in sweat when one fighter took a good punch to the face. Thankfully I had a bit of time to practice before Andy and Errol were on."

Indeed, he got a few really decent shots, which I was able to use in the paper. Getting there had been a mission. I didn't have a car and we went up in Kev's Hillman Imp, the rad boiling dry every few miles, so we'd have to stop and refill it with water from bottles we'd taken with us. We followed the old Roman road, the A5, which had plenty of pull-ins. It had been a good call to avoid the M1.

Andy was held to a draw by Ian Lazarus, a south-paw from Leeds, while Errol stopped Vince Gajny, from Stratford-upon Avon, not long into the second round of their super-middleweight bout.

I once drove from Stevenage to Halifax to watch Straughny fight. It was April 1985, and he was facing the experienced Curaçao-born Tom Collins, from Leeds, known as The Bomb. But Collins was The Dud that night: Andy defused him. Terry Greenaway came along to keep me company on the drive. It was a 350-mile round-trip – but it was all over in just 36 seconds, including the 10-second count.

A lot of these fights were televised on ITV and Andy would get a tape and nip to Terry's house in Stevenage to go through the action for some pointers on how to improve. The Collins fight was on April 18 and, having hardly broken sweat, he was back in action just six days later, on the Wednesday, against an American, Roosevelt Green, knocking him out in six in Shoreditch, which I also watched.

Andy recalls: "On the Saturday, I took some videos over to Terry's. I got there about 10am but his wife Ann had found him dead in the bathroom – it is something that will always stay with me. I still miss him now." Andy took many heavy blows in bouts. But this one was below the belt, for sure.

10 Rocky roads

I saw many fights at Wembley when I worked in west
London on the Slough and Hounslow Evening
Mail and lived in Alperton, down the road from the
arena.

John L Gardner was touted as the next "great white
hope" among the heavyweights. We'd had Jack Bod-
ell, Richard Dunn and Joe Bugner, but they all fell
short of world title standard.

Retired journalist and author Norman Giller was
Gardner's publicist and tried to sell him as the next

Rocky Marciano. It was a tough task. "I organised a picture of him in bed with a photo of Marciano alongside the alarm clock, which the papers lapped up," Norman recalls. But, sadly, he wasn't the next Rocky.

John L (the L stood for Lewis) had a fight lined up with Muhammad Ali in Hawaii in the spring of 1981. But Ali, who was approaching 40 and had just been stopped for the first time, by Larry Holmes in Las Vegas, was not granted a licence. Gardner had done well in a three-round exhibition against Ali a few years earlier and said: "I really believed I could beat him. I'd be too busy for him in his old age."

With Gardner, known as The Hackney Rock, you always had the impression that in the face of every opponent he saw his abusive dad. "I never wanted to be a champion," said the man who went on win British, Commonwealth and European belts. "But I did want a bit of respect."

I covered his British and Commonwealth title fight at Wembley in late June 1979, against Paul Sykes, a spiky character who spent years in prison for a slew of violent offences.

For a preview, I phoned Henry Cooper – at his greengrocer's shop in Wembley. Our 'Enery was charming – and in no hurry to stop talking about boxing and get back to his spuds. Yet it seemed an incongruous setting for such an iconic British sportsman. Henry ran the shop with another Henry Cooper (no relation) whom he had met on holiday. It was a financial flop. As his manager, Jim Wicks, said to him about the venture: "What the bleedin' 'ell d'you know about vegetables? You think cauli-flowers grow on ears!"

Sykes' life was a litany of alcohol abuse, petty robberies, violent crime and prison. He had been fast-tracked to a British title attempt – this was only his ninth bout – but he couldn't handle Gardner. The fight was stopped when Sykes briefly turned his back, which was never his style out of the ring. He once took on four nightclub bouncers and came a very decent second but cut his eye, costing him a payday fight against Lennie McLean, of Lock, Stock and Two Smoking Barrels movie fame. Lennie, who played a heavy in that cult Guy Ritchie flick, never did much like "northern monkeys"...

Cooper had correctly called the result in my preview, predicting that Gardner's all-action, swarming style would be too much for the powerful, bullying Sykes. It was "Easy as ABC for John L", our paper proclaimed the next day.

I was fortunate to see some brilliant displays from British boxers in what seemed like a golden age, if not at heavyweight. In July 1980, I watched Maurice Hope beat Rocky Mattioli at Wembley to retain the WBC super-welter title he won from the Italian in San Remo a year earlier. Hope, who at one point tried to become manager of Errol Christie, stopped Mattioli in round 11 of 15 but lost his crown a year later to the legendary Bronx-born Puerto Rican, Wilfredo Benitez, in Las Vegas.

I always enjoyed watching the 'Fenland Tiger' –

Dave 'Boy' Green. He never won a world title but the welterweight opposition of the time included Carlos Palomino and Sugar Ray Leonard. Green was out cold before he hit the deck in the fourth against Leonard in Maryland. The boy from Chatteris, near Wisbech, retired in 1982 after a 41-contest career with only four defeats.

One of the best bouts I saw from ringside was Jim Watt's bruising world lightweight clash against the hard-as-nails Nicaraguan, Alexis Arguello. Watt was decked in the seventh, bloodied in the ninth and then lost a unanimous decision. Watt had battled grittily to the final bell despite savage cuts to his lip and eyes. He said afterwards: "I have a car business in Scotland and if I had to do an estimate on my face now, I would probably write it off."

As with football, I largely stopped going to live boxing after I moved into newspaper production, working evening and weekend shifts. But I still took a keen interest. One of my big heroes was Muhammad Ali and there was one opportunity I could not pass up when my wife Pam and I went to stay in Indiana with my brother Kevin and his wife Bridget in Indiana in 2018.

Kev planned a day trip for us, over the state border to Louisville, Kentucky, and I asked if we could visit the Muhammad Ali Centre. He took little persuasion and even Pam, who has been known to enjoy boxing, found it fascinating. But it is so much more than a boxing museum. It delves into Ali's controversies: refusing to fight for his country in Vietnam and his long civil rights struggles, his conversion to Islam. It has brilliant sections devoted to racial prejudice and the social history of black America, with films of civil rights campaigners Dr Martin Luther King and Malcolm X.

It is easy to forget how much Ali achieved after his retirement from the ring as a humanitarian and philanthropist. Those parts are as fascinating as all the on-demand fight footage, which you can watch sitting at ringside, surrounded by myriad dressing gowns, gloves, posters and medals.

On one wall is an oddly low-key exhibit - a framed replacement for the Olympic gold medal that Ali, then known by his birth name, Cassius Clay, is said to have lobbed off the city's Second Street Bridge into the Ohio River after returning from the Rome Games in 1960, thinking his success for his country would enable him to sidestep the awful racial bigotry of the time in America's South. It didn't.

The truth of that incident became blurred with time – did he toss the medal or didn't he? Ali was happy to keep the waters muddied. But the replacement was a wonderful and fitting gesture. And who can forget him lighting the Olympic flame at the Atlanta Games, fighting hard to steady his shakes as he battled Parkinson's Disease.

Some of the less prominent things resonated most for me, such as a photo of Ali making a young boy's day by stopping his car to sign an autograph. He was a man of many talents and many kindnesses.

For me, Ali is the greatest sportsman the world has

known. I recently re-watched one of his TV interviews with Michael Parkinson and he was so eloquent on the way black people are treated, asking in the most disarming way, a glint in his eye, why so many characters in stories and cartoons and popular culture are white.

Events in mid-2020, with unrest worldwide over the death of unarmed George Floyd in police custody, sparking the Black Lives Matter protests, shows there is still a very long way to go in the campaign for racial equality. They would have brought out the fighter in Ali.

I know that Andy Straughn, for one, shares my view of Ali... he named his son, an aspiring boxer, Cassius.

11 Graham Poll only booked me once

As kids, our Wembley was somewhat different from the one you see on TV. Doubtless millions of other young boys the world over have had their own version. Shephalbury Park in Stevenage was ours, a brilliant space, where my friends and I would spend pretty much every spare hour of daylight, kicking a football, playing cricket – or just hanging out until a weary parent would drag us home for dinner or bedtime.

A street lamp near the swings served as our floodlight when games went on late. Major tournaments or club rivalries would be settled there – even if it was just a group of pals with a patched-up plastic ball, several previous punctures repaired by having small bits of plastic, possibly from the last "dead" ball, melted over the hole. The swings were behind the goal of our chosen pitch which, by chance, later became our Sunday League team's home pitch. Further across were four more pitches and a tidy wood and brick pavilion, where teams changed and which was the domain of Bill Robinson, the cheery park-keeper we used to help by putting up and bringing back the goal nets and corner flags when we had games. The dressing rooms were always clean, even for kids' matches in the afternoon when adults with muddy boots had trashed the place in the morning.

Being the smallest on our team, I was designated net putter-upper, perched uneasily on a centre-half's shoulders, usually our skipper Dave Amies, unsteadily plonking them over hooks on the cross-bar and kicking net pegs into often frozen ground. If we were lucky, we got a loan of the one mallet. You needed a keen sense of balance, which also helped when evading lunging challenges on a Sunday morning.

I was sometimes known to dish them out, too, often slyly, so the traffic wasn't entirely one way. A favourite bit of goalmouth chicanery I'd picked up from reading about Italian football was to accidentally stand on a defender's foot when a cross came in. It stopped them jumping.

I was only ever booked once – by Graham Poll, the man who went to be the country's top Premier League ref. Famously, at the 2014 World Cup finals, he booked the Croatian, Josip Simunic, during the match against Australia not once, or twice, but three times before sending him off, confusing him with a team-mate.

Graham, who is from Stevenage and for a decade was the country's best referee, admitted to having 'brain fog'. A costly one, too – he had been in line for the game's biggest honour, refereeing the World Cup final itself. But it was snatched from him and must have been utterly devastating.

Looking back, I was probably guilty of being over-forceful in a sliding challenge, though I did connect squarely with the ball. The player sprawling his full length was merely a consequence of my momentum. These days, though, it might have warranted less a yellow than a straight red as I could have been judged to be not in control.

The best days were those spent in the park. I'd walk up, football in hand – until I reached the hole in the hedge. That was my Wembley tunnel. I'd balance the ball on my thigh, like Bobby Moore, or Spurs hero Alan Mullery (after Jimmy Greaves left for West Ham), striding out before a big game and emerging onto the "stadium". I would then boot the ball skywards to the roars of an enthusiastic but imaginary crowd. I remember getting my socks sodden from morning dew and feeling the ground crunch from number of crisp, early Spring frosts.

Yet the weather seldom put us off. Only once, on a youth club tour to Norway with Letchworth FC, did I actually play in front of something resembling a crowd.

Before Sunday games, the lads would be working out if they needed moulded boots or be busy fiddling with screw-in studs. There was always a lot of banter and B.O. And strapping for creaky ankles and dodgy knees. There would be chat about which pubs had been visited the night before and, once, the adventures of bailing a particular player out of nick in the small hours.

Growing up, I had pictures on my bedroom wall, mostly of Spurs players – Jimmy Greaves, Martin Chivers, Alan Gilzean and Pat Jennings, all of whom I was fortunate to meet in later years. But I also had posters of foreign stars such as Pele, Eusebio, and Franz Beckenbauer. Sometimes I chose pictures, cut mostly from Shoot! Magazine, simply because I liked the kits, like the sky blue with dark blue trim of Coventry, the old gold of Wolves or the brilliant single red diagonal stripe on white shirt of Peru, an all-time classic beloved by many around the globe.

I also used to organise the league ladders Shoot! gave away free at the start of the season – all four divisions plus the Scottish. I'd grab dad's paper and re-order the teams after that weekend's round of matches.

There were a good many teams in my well-used Subbuteo collection, too. It was a relatively modest one – no Wembley-style accoutrements other than a scoreboard and a scale-size FA Cup complete with detachable lid. The Spurs team was astonishingly accurate in detail: my Dave Mackay broke his legs twice, just like the fiery Scot in real life. They also won my FA Cup quite often. Not that it was fixed, though I might be playing against myself and doing the match commentary.

I didn't need telling that I wasn't going to make it as a footballer: I was too small. OK not small enough to make a Subbuteo line-up. But it still hurt to be rejected at first sight by the coach of a junior side that a mate of mine joined. I decided then that I would look to enjoy my football, no matter what level I played. It was mostly modest but with the odd moment to look back on with pride: a few cup wins and final defeats, and some games at big grounds, such as Crystal Palace's Selhurst Park and Luton's Kenilworth Road.

One of the best game I recall was a 4-4 draw with Hitchin Italian – a bunch of lads from the restaurant trade. It was played in such a great competitive but friendly spirit from start to finish, something even the referee remarked upon afterwards.

I loved the inter-house matches at junior school because we got to wear the brilliant school team colours – old gold and grey quarters or blue and white quarters. Proper shirts! The mob games in the playground at lunch closely resembled the famous annual Ashbourne Shrovetide matches, only with more thuggery. Sore and grazed knees were badges of honour in class each afternoon. I usually spent my time out on the wing, largely ignored but screaming for the ball in acres of space.

My first proper team football was for a youth club, Bowes-Lyon. I had the idea then that I was a sweeper. They were all the rage in the early 70s. The centre back would do all the heavy contact stuff and the sweeper would pick up the loose ball and either lash it to safety or start an attack with an astute pass. I did get half decent at it. We went on an end-of-season tour to Holland and we even fielded a girls' team – long before their game took off. I seem to think they did better than we did.

I graduated to men's football with a Saturday team, Marley Flooring... quite apt, because most of the lads played like they'd spent the previous night on the tiles. My first chance came as a sub, up front. Straight on, I dummied a known local hard man, John Batcheldor, on the halfway line and would have been through on goal had he not he cut me off at the waist. It would have been a red card now, no messing, and could even have been viewed as a common assault, but he never even got booked. Irony of ironies, John later became a referee – a very decent one, too. True poacher turned gamekeeper.

I made a few guest appearances for Letchworth Youth, notably on a tour to Kristiansand, Norway. Our main weapon was a striker called Imre Varadi. He was a proper footballer: he made it at Everton and also played for Sheffield Wednesday and Leeds United. Imre would bang in hat-tricks seemingly at will and whenever we were in trouble, the plan was just to get the ball to him. He was a powerhouse. And quick. I was mates with his brother, Tony, who was in the team but a bit more trouble - and no slouch with the ladies. In that department he was Premier League to my Vauxhall Conference.

With experience of playing, I worked out that it would be better for me to use my relative speed off the mark and ability to avoid being battered by opposition heavies out wide, initially as a winger and then, as I got older and slowed down, as a full-back. I probably played some of my best football at right back.

It was with the No2 on my back that I won a trophy with Stevenage Casuals, who used to drink in the Mutual Friend pub, where I worked part-time when I was at college. Their regular full-back, Sam, broke his leg and I stepped in for him for the rest of the season. We were losing the final but pulled off a 3-2 victory that we celebrated back at 'work'. I offered him my medal afterwards but he refused to take it.

I seldom played on Saturdays, because of work commitments and came to regret one time that I did, guesting for the local bus staff team at the invitation of a mate. I scored early on then got clattered badly from behind. I got through the rest of the game but when I got back to the dressing room found I could not bend to get my boots off. My mate had to do it for me.

Next day I limped to the hospital, across from where I was living, and found I had a damaged pancreas. It was Christmas in hospital – a week in all – and it made me realise how hard the nurses worked. Apart from a few hamstrings and bashed knees, and also some cracked ribs on one occasion, I got off relatively unscathed from a couple of decades of organised sport.

With the pro career a non-runner, I pursued one that brought me as close to the game as possible – without getting taken out at the waist for my troubles. As a reporter, I reasoned, you'd get the best seat in the house – and someone would actually pay you for the privilege. What was not to like?

The time that I spent writing about sport, before I moved into office-based production work, got me some very enviable seats – ringside at world-title boxing, in the press box at FA Cup Finals and England internationals at the old Wembley, the tennis at Wimbledon, Test match cricket at Lord's – and even inside the ropes at a Ryder Cup golf at The Belfry, where I got to meet a big idol, Nick Faldo.

Brentford, Chelsea, Fulham and QPR were my regular haunts when I was on the Evening Mail in west London. I was sent to meet Tommy Docherty when he became manager at QPR and he was dressed in just a towel when I was ushered inside at their training ground in west London to meet him. "I said: 'Should I have brought my towel? I didn't realise your office was a Turkish bath'."

We got on pretty well after that. A couple of mornings a week I'd ring him at his hotel in Holland Park Avenue for the team news and his views on topical issues. He was a likeable rogue who had been forced out of Manchester United because of his affair with Mary Brown, the United physio's wife. Opposing fans would wind the Doc up by singing: "Who's Up Mother Brown?". Tommy died on New Year's Eve, 2020.

When I was covering sport in the flesh, I exchanged my childhood Wembley for the actual one; the 1923-vintage version with the old twin towers, which I had only previously visited on school trips to watch a couple of schoolboy internationals. This level of privileged access brought the occasional brush with childhood heroes – and some odd coincidences.

Reporting for the Stevenage paper, I was having a comfort break at half-time in an England schools' game and became aware of someone arriving just to my left. I glanced across - and it took a quick repeat look to confirm that it really was Bobby Moore.

He nodded and got on with what gents do in such places. I would like to report that, as he did before greeting the Queen after winning the World Cup in 1966, the great man wiped his hands on a velvet cloth ahead of daintily shaking hands with me – but it was altogether more mundane, and hygienic.

England were playing Scotland in May 1978 and Bobby had not long retired as a player. Porn mag king David Sullivan made him sports editor of the Sunday Sport, though his reports were "ghost-written" for him. I was there because a local lad, Shaun Brooks, was captain of the England side. As we walked back to the press box, which was accessed by a vertigo-inspiring walkway to the gantry that hung just below the roof, Bobby said it was always a joy to be back at a place he considered his second football home. There were so many happy memories for him. He won the FA Cup and European Cup-winners' Cup at the stadium with West Ham in 1964 and 1965 before collecting the Jules Rimet trophy a year later. That was of course the most famous day in English football – yet he said he seldom dwelt on it. I said I would have dined out on it for eternity!

Bobby offered a ready opinion on Shaun, who he said looked "like a man in a boys' match" and was someone who had a definite future in the game. Headline sorted: "England World Cup-winning captain tips Shaun for pro future", and the rest wrote itself.

Bobby knew that Shaun's dad Johnny had played for Spurs, been capped for England and was a gifted midfield player. But he tempered his prediction by saying a boy of Shaun's natural talent might find it hard to rise to the very top in a game that increasingly put work-rate ahead of creative craft and the ability to influence a game from central midfield. Shaun would not be the last to suffer at that altar.

He joined Crystal Palace to become part of Terry Venables' young side that was hyped up by the media as the "Team of the Eighties". Palace were being touted as the great new hope to knock the all-conquering Liverpool team off their perch, based around a crop of young players who won two successive FA Youth Cups – the first to do so since Matt Busby's "Babes" at Manchester United in the 1950s.

It was an impossible label to live up to. But these Super Eagles boasted a future England left-back, Kenny Sampson, and a prodigious teenage winger, Vince Hilaire, who is still spoken of with reverence at Selhurst Park. Beside them were more experienced older hands such as Gerry Francis (an England captain in the making), David Swindlehurst and Steve Kember. And they did briefly top the old First Division table.

Palace's captain and centre-half, Jim Cannon, has since reflected that the team's promise was brittle and inevitably went unfulfilled. "The time to name someone Team of the Eighties was 1989 – not 1979," he said. Too many of the players in that team believed their own publicity and that, combined with a titanic drinking culture, snuffed out these 'Babes' in their infancy.

Shaun made his first-team debut for Palace against Leeds United in April 1980. He was only 17 (still too young to drink legally). As the Eagles plummeted, his career suffered collateral damage, but he played 54 times for the south London club before joining Leyton Orient for the first of two spells. He also played for Bournemouth, where he was later an academy coach there.

His dad was a wonderful character. When I first saw Johnny, he was playing for Stevenage Town in the Southern League. He was a touch of class in a tough, physical league where you didn't get time on the ball – you got whacked. He always made his own time and space, as the very best do.

John was not the quickest, except when it came to his speed of thought. Years later, in his mid-50s, he was still playing Stevenage Sunday League football, for Knebworth Sports Club. I played against him a couple of times and still have nightmares about how he sat me down in the centre circle with just a couple of swivels of his hips! We'd joke about it whenever I saw him coming off the packed London train. He'd say I always seemed to find a seat – on a busy train, or on the football pitch.

Shaun did not go on to win full England caps like his dad. Instead, after a 380-game career with Palace, Leyton Orient and Bournemouth, he did his coaching badges. The last time I saw a photo of him, though, he was his dad's image. A veritable chip off the old block.

And his passage through the game showed Bobby Moore's judgment at that chance meeting at Wembley all those years ago to be very sound indeed.

12 Glenda

In 1978, I was deputy sports editor of the Evening Mail in Uxbridge and we got press tickets for all the big events at Wembley – the stadium and the Arena. Football was always the biggest thrill, walking up to the famous twin towers, with the sounds and smells as food vendors and scarf and programme sellers plied their trade along Wembley Way, and the fans warmed up their voices.

To reach the press box, you had to go in through an area that was always packed before any match with famous faces – a mix of former players, celebs and other invited guests. There would be cacophony of chinking glasses and rattling cutlery as you made your way to the lift. The walls were adorned with photos of moments from the stadium's history – including speedway and greyhound racing, which took place there for many years.

Whenever I sat in that press box, my eyes would be drawn to the giant scoreboard. The image of hat-trick hero Geoff Hurst's World Cup-winning goal in 1966 was seared in my mind – and that scoreboard spelled out the story of that historic afternoon. The giant letters and numbers would be slotted into place by someone perched on that precarious plat-form – a thought that would chill me, as someone with no head for heights; I got vertigo wearing those awful ankle-breaking platform shoes or scaling a double-height kerb.

As a Spurs fan, it was a highlight to have been there the night Glenn Hoddle made his long-awaited Eng-land debut, against Bulgaria in 1979. Both nights, in fact. The game was postponed on the Wednesday evening because of thick fog. The postponement meant, however, that Kevin Keegan had to miss the game as he was needed back in Germany for a club game with Hamburg.

The visibility was not the best even at the second time of asking. But I had a clear view of Hoddle's brilliant, side-footed half-volley from outside the box. It was a precision strike. Wembley erupted, with the fans feeling they were in at the birth of a true international talent, fit to rival any top French-man or Brazilian – someone who could coax the team back to international glory.

Hoddle – unkindly labelled by some critics as "Glenda" because he wasn't a scrapper – also made the opening goal, for Dave Watson, as England won 2-0 in a European Championships qualifier. It was an altogether impressive introduction.

The silky midfielder would go on to play only 53 times for his country but later manage the national team. France legend Michel Platini claimed 53 caps was a travesty and Hoddle "would have won 150 caps had he been born French".

But Hoddle never had the confidence of his manager, the poker-faced, pragmatist Ron Greenwood, who repeatedly picked then discarded a player considered to be the most naturally gifted of his era. Greenwood had been chosen for the job as a safe pair of hands – ironic in that he couldn't decide between his two best goalkeepers, Ray Clemence and Peter Shilton. The former West Ham boss got the job when Don Revie decamped to the Middle East in return for a mountain of cash. But Greenwood would never deliver success in a major tournament, the yardstick by which England managers are judged.

I felt that Greenwood resented the press clamour for certain players to be included in his side. After that sparkling debut, Hoddle was left out of the next three line-ups. Only twice did he play two in a row under his management. Hoddle was used only once at the 1982 World Cup in Spain. He was in his prime, at 25, yet his manager still labelled him "one for the future" and something of a luxury item.

Little wonder, with that sort of thinking, that England lost their way in world football between 1970 and 1986. One wonders what they might have achieved with Hoddle as the centrepiece and the equally maverick Brian Clough as manager. Cloughie, the people's choice for the job, was seen by those in charge at the Football Association as being too outspoken – an undiplomatic motor-mouth. He was driven by a huge ego but he was a winner. Taking Nottingham Forest from the game's second tier to twice being European champions is a feat that is hard to imagine ever being equalled.

On one of my next visits to Wembley, I got up close and very personal with the FA Cup. So I know exactly where I was on that bright, hot afternoon of May 12, 1979. It was Arsenal v Manchester United in what is remembered as the "five-minute Cup Final". Arsenal led through a Brian Talbot goal, and Frank Stapleton doubled the Gunners' lead before half time. It was pretty routine stuff, with the Londoners coasting to victory – until the last few minutes, when the game went potty.

Gordon McQueen pulled one back for United and, when Sammy McIlroy wriggled through to equalise moments later, it seemed certain that extra-time was on the way – if United didn't capitalise on their momentum to win it. But then Arsenal midfielder Alan Sunderland swept the ball home at the far post, in the dying seconds after some Liam Brady magic, to complete the drama and clutch victory for the Gunners from the jaws of embarrassment.

I did not have to file any words until the Monday but, with deadlines looming and so much action to catch up with, the press box was a hive of activity as the Sunday reporters did hasty rewrites and bashed their reports out on portable typewriters before reading their copy over the phone to their offices.

I took a slow walk down to where the post-match interviews would take place but got lost in a labyrinth of by now empty staircases that all looked the same. At the bottom, I emerged into a wide area where a couple of coaches were parked, one behind the other. To my right I could see the pitch. I had come out in the players' tunnel.

As I rounded the front coach, I saw the yellow-shirted Arsenal midfielder Brian Talbot. He was sitting on a canvas chair outside the dressing room with the Cup on his lap – and a faraway look of satisfaction.

I was tempted to grab a proper word with him but instead mumbled something inane like: "That's rather nice. You taking it home?!" He replied: "Oh yes!!" and tightened his bear-like grip around what at the time was still one of world football's most coveted trophies.

Professionally, I might have tried to get an exclusive line out of him – but it didn't feel right on a human level. I sensed I would have intruded on a special, private moment.

He was, I thought, reflecting on a unique achievement – winning the trophy for the second successive year with separate clubs. In 1978, it had been for Ipswich – against Arsenal. He did enough for the East Anglian side to earn a £450,000 move to Highbury in January 1979, just in time for the Gunners' FA Cup run that season.

At the press conference, Brian said pretty much what he might have told me anyway. "It was nice in my first season at Arsenal to play such a part in winning a big game like that. I remember a lot more the second time round. Last year, the occasion went by me, so I tried to absorb a lot more this time."

When I heard this, I felt reassured that I had done the right thing by leaving him to savour his glory. He would be back at Wembley a year later – making it three in a row – but Arsenal lost that final to West Ham and Trevor Brooking's stooping header. There was a postscript to this 15 years later, when I was editing match programmes for Stevenage Borough. Brian was then manager of Rushden & Diamonds and I spoke to him ahead of a Vauxhall Conference clash at Boro.

He was really helpful and chatty, one of the more personable ones to deal with – I asked him to cast his mind back to that Wembley afternoon in 1979. He recalled having a quiet moment with the trophy – but had no recall of our fleeting conversation. That is as it should be: just a man sitting out of the hot sun, drenched with sweat, with a large, world-famous old silver pot on his lap, reflecting on a precious personal moment.

I had a ticket a week or so later for the England-Scotland match at Wembley but couldn't go.

I had the pitiful excuse that I was getting married that afternoon, just as they were kicking off just up the road from Perivale, o the A40. As we checked into our honeymoon hotel that evening, up the road from Wembley, my bride, Maggie, (still in her dress) and I were greeted by a group of boisterous, tired and emotional tartan-bedecked fans, chorusing: "Dirty weekend!"

My last press box outing there was the Spurs v Arsenal Cup semi-final in 1991, which was illuminated by Paul Gascoigne's heart-stopping long-range free-kick that embarrassed goalkeeper David Seaman.

There had been tickets going begging at The Mail on Sunday, where I was working, because the game had been moved to the Sunday for a TV audience. I went with Bob Rosson, from our art desk – he was an Arsenal fan and, like me, didn't get out much!

When Gazza scored, I think I almost caught Bob in the face as I leapt out of my seat, before quickly remembering where I was. Bob was a bit more guarded when Gary Lineker scored his second of the match to wrap up a 3-1 win – but I did at least tone down the gloating until we were back in the office the next week.

13 Street of Shame

The first time I went to Fleet Street was nothing to do with work. I was on a college business diploma course, doing an English project on newspapers, and the Daily Mirror offered me a tour of their offices in High Holborn. I got to see the newsroom and print room and came home armed with bits of metal type, some page proofs, an Andy Capp cartoon book and a copy of the paper as souvenirs – plus a fired-up ambition to work in the industry. I can still recall the smell of molten metal and the din in the print room.

The news floor was abuzz with phones ringing,

a cacophony of typewriters, and the odd shouted instruction. And no, that didn't include "hold the front page".

When the Mail announced it was to bring out a Sunday paper in May 1982, my friend Danny John tipped me off. His mum, Patsy, was to be the sports desk assistant and, she said that if I wrote in for a casual job she could nudge my letter towards the top of the pile.

I got a regular shift each Saturday, sub-editing sports results, and I have never forgotten the kindness Patsy did me, with the doors it opened for me. That first step is all-important. When I got a full-time job on the paper a decade later, one of my first priorities was to take her out for a decent lunch, at the Orangery in Kensington Gardens.

Patsy was always a good source of office gossip and had reams of anecdotes from her time in the industry. She was a great teller of "war" stories. She was offered her job at the new Mail on Sunday (MoS) by Alan Hubbard, who had been appointed sports editor. "We had worked on the James Goldsmith-owned news magazine 'Now' which had survived barely two years," said Patsy.

"Alan was chief sports writer and I worked on the news desk. I had been with Associated Newspapers before – for the Daily Sketch, Daily Mail and Evening News. With 'Now' magazine known as 'Then' magazine, because it failed, I had seen three title closures.

"When I first walked into the MoS newsroom, a group of news subs I knew saw me. One said, 'well that's it, lads. Might as well call it a day and put our coats on and go home. Look who's just come in: the Albatross of Fleet Street!'." Patsy's reputation wasn't helped when, a few years later, she left the MoS to join Robert Maxwell's new sports magazine, Sportsweek. Guess what happened to that...

I was by now sports editor on the Gazette in North Herts, so working MoS shifts would present a con-undrum: how could I sell the idea to my boss of working elsewhere on the busiest sports day of the week? I spun it that if I worked locally on Sundays we could widen our coverage.

Hugh Bateson, my brilliant deputy, who worked for many years on the Independent and now the Daily Telegraph, covered Saturdays. It meant I took in athletics, rugby and cricket as well as ice hockey and table tennis (we had national league teams in both) and had the chance to press more community flesh. Sports that would otherwise have been content to send in their own reports thus got higher profile coverage. But I still owe Hugh several drinks for his support.

The Mail group is based today in Kensington High Street, above Barkers department store, but back then was in old Northcliffe House, off the south side of Fleet Street. I was nervous but excited when I did my first shift and didn't fully appreciate the signifi-cance of the event – or, until much later, how the project almost foundered in just a matter of weeks.

We did three weeks' training and dry-runs, though they never printed a complete dummy edition, which with hindsight was probably much regretted upstairs. It was the first national Sunday newspaper launch in 21 years and yet it appeared doomed from the off and was viewed by media insiders as a massive flop.

To save costs, there was no colour supplement, when its main rivals all had one. There were printing nightmares as we fell half a million copies short of the print target for that first issue, which ran to 64 pages. Then there was the content.

Britain was only recently at war with Argentina and, while the editor, Bernard Shrimsley, led the paper with news of a bombing mission on the Falklands – "Our Day!", the front page proclaimed – the news coverage was underwhelming and the sports coverage was also panned. The back-page lead was, bizarrely, a report of a roller-hockey international between England and Argentina, which took place in Holland. It is a sport the paper has, I am quite sure, never featured since. Football, our national game, didn't get a sniff as the splash.

In just six weeks, the initial 1.2 million sales plummeted to just 700,000. Drastic action was needed if it was not to add to Patsy's reputation as a harbinger of doom – and see millions invested in the project flushed down the drain.

Shrimsley was fired, in person, by Vere Harmsworth, whose trusted right-hand man David English, editor of the Daily Mail, then led a "task force" – a term over-used at that time – of journos from the Daily Mail in a move likened by MoS staffers to the

SAS swinging in through the windows, locked and loaded.

English did, however, stop the rot. His new part-works, including You magazine, transformed the paper's fortunes, winning over readers and advertisers, and a new full-time editor, Stewart Steven, oversaw its speedy upward trajectory. Yet at his first board meeting, Stewart had heard the paper was projected to lose £24 million in its first year – and there were some in that meeting of the view that Vere should cut and run.

Conspiracy theorists on the MoS had it that the Daily Mail coup had been planned all along, with pressure to take the paper in a certain direction, knowing it would go pear-shaped and they could then ride in as white knights. I am not sure how much credence to give to those theories but newspaper offices are Machiavellian places.

I recall reporters hiding their best stories until Saturday morning because if they were put out there too early, their tales would get shot down and never see the light of day. Instead they would float some readily expendable idea early on. There was the constant fear for them that senior execs would take all the credit for their best ideas –the sort of power politics goes on widely.

I've also seen many high-ranking news execs think they had won the lottery by getting fired for some spurious reason – perhaps their face didn't fit. They would shuffle off with a security guard and a bin bag – only to turn up at a rival paper in some other well-paid role within days or weeks, and having pocketed a huge severance cheque. I remember Brian Alexander, who was a good sports editor, and a decent bloke, saying how he was standing in the urinals one morning when the boss came in beside him. He looked across and said to Brian: "It's not working out, is it? Come and see me later and we will sort out a package for you."

Ker-ching: that was the mortgage or burdensome school fees paid. Some were lucky enough to repeat the trick a few times. Failing upwards, they call it. Not so with Brian, who, despite an unfortunate stammer, did well on radio.

Stewart Steven made the Mail on Sunday radically different from the Daily. That was his talent. It became a paper that would set the following week's news agenda and not become a Daily Mail Mini-Me. He hired big-name columnists and aligned the title's politics closer to the centre – another clear distinction from the Daily – though he fell short of exhorting readers to vote SDP (the new party set up by four Labour rebels, including former Stevenage MP Shirley Williams, that later merged with the Liberal Party to form the LibDems).

A few years later, when I joined full-time to work in an editorial systems team set up to bring computers to journalists' desks, it was Stewart Steven who rubber-stamped my hiring. I had to have this medical for insurance purposes - apparently if I died while on the job, as it were, my widow would be seriously in the money. It was not nice to know I was worth more dead than alive and started viewing her cooking with more suspicion that usual!

Stewart was also my first "customer" when we brought in Macintosh computers. I got him, and Executive Editor Jim Anderson doing most of a day's training which consisted of a couple of hours' playing Tetris, to get used to using a mouse for the first time, followed by an overview of what his staff would be doing with all this expensive kit we'd got him to sign off. I also had to install one of these new-fangled machines at Stewart's home in Chiswick (I think he was writing a book). It was an ocean of calm and you would not know you were in a throbbing metropolis.

The boss was a rarity among editors in that he knew where the sports department was (just outside our systems office). He was very much a rugby union and cricket man, though. So many editors, in my experience, are dismissive of the "games department", forgetting how many people buy the paper for its sports coverage – and the paper was very good at it after that poor start. They used to joke that certain editors who came to visit needed to tie a rope round their waist so they could find their way back to their office.

One of our jobs was to support freelancers and guest columnists and you found out thing you never imagined. For instance, Adam Faith, the 60s pop idol and actor, wrote a City share-tipping column for the paper. He was by all accounts stonkingly wealthy and yet every week he'd drop by our office to cadge free AA batteries. I am not sure they were exclusively for his Tandy, as they seemed to run forever on Duracells.

It was tempting to ask Tel (his real name was Terry Nelhams and he preferred not to go by his stage name) 'What Do You Want If You Don't Want Money?' when he swung by. But we always knew what he wanted. Packs of batteries.

He made his name in the early 60s with a string of hits, including two No.1s ,but as his star waned he reinvented himself as an actor, starring in the TV show Budgie, playing a Cockney ex-con. He also starred in a couple of decent movies – as David Essex's manager in Stardust, and alongside Roger Daltrey in McVicar. His switch to being a financial pundit was not nearly so successful. He himself went bust, owing £30m after his investment in a TV Money Channel bombed. He had heart surgery in 1986 and died from a heart attack while touring with a stage production in Stoke in 2003.

Down the years we had brilliant sportswriters such as the multi-award-winning Patrick Collins (who was on board from the start) and some big-name (and highly-paid) guest columnists such as Sir Bobby Robson, Glenn Hoddle and Gary Neville – though anyone who has had to edit Neville's "pearls" might take issue with that. The former Manchester United defender-turned-TV pundit always believed his stuff was too important to be constrained to a single page, and wanted his words untouched and to write his own headlines – despite, of course, having no knowledge of typefaces or how many letters you can cram across a page.

The sports desk at the MoS before the move to Kensington High Street was at the far end of the newsroom. Behind them sat the team of all-male copytakers. Staff in the field would phone across their words and these guys would type them up. They were experienced, fast and knowledgeable – and not to be messed with. That corridor led to a door, behind which were the cashiers: very important people to be nurtured. Expenses and, in some cases, wages were still paid in cash.

One afternoon, a reporter tried to make his way to cashiers but found the door locked and barred and banging noises coming from the other side. You don't come between a reporter and his expenses – so a few of them were soon busy trying to force the door open, Patsy John recalls.

"When they made it through, they found the cashiers had been victims of an attempted robbery. The other entrance was from the street. The armed, would-be robbers had tied up the staff, who had been banging loudly, trying to attract attention.

I believe the gang escaped with very little and, although here was a story right on our doorstep, everyone was more concerned at getting their expenses than writing it up."

Trevor Bond, the Associate Sports Editor, was one of the kindest people I worked with. He loved a drop of the amber nectar, though, and I remember quick breaks with him in The Harrow, in Whitefriars

Street, all too literally – and too often – stumbling distance from the office. He'd have a large Scotch and American: but that tiny bottle of ginger ale was everlasting. He would put in the tiniest amount before it would have the metal top eased back on and it would sit on a shelf behind the bar ready for his next visit.

For a long time, Trev thought nobody knew he didn't only partake of a drink outside the office – we were all wise enough not to pick up his coffee or tea by mistake. When under the influence, though, he was never offensive, he'd just repeat himself, often three times: "I'll have a scotch, I'll have a scotch, I'll have a scotch." It really was trebles all round.

This was a very different era, when strong drink went down at every opportunity, and long breaks – a three-hour lunch was not unheard of – were almost like badges of honour. I think in Systems we once managed to stretch one lunch out to just shy of four hours. But Phil Jordan, our boss, who later decamped to the States, was a pro in every sense. He knew his stuff, was well read and connected, had been a very good reporter and knew the boundaries – and how we could push them.

He introduced me to the CQ, or Conference Quickie, when you'd nip out for a livener while the execs were holding the morning news meeting. There followed the epic, drink-sodden lunch, interspersed with something to eat and paid for with his Lordship's expenses; then possibly an "early one", which was a swift night-cap before you headed for your train.

There were tales of people extending the early one into an "out out" situation, eventually falling asleep on said train and missing their stop. One certain cricket writer once unknowingly spent the night in the sidings. I never quite managed that but do recall speaking into the great white telephone at length on a couple of journeys back from King's Cross.

Stewart Steven saw the value of sports in helping office team-building. We had cricket matches and golf trips, including one memorable one to Ireland, when we played Portmarnock, just outside Dublin – in my case very badly – and, at St Margarets, even worse.

He hosted a cricket match at a posh country house estate in Buckinghamshire one year and the former England spinners John Emburey and Phil Edmonds were drafted in as guests – Phil for the editor's team and John for ours. I had the misfortune to unintentionally run out crime reporter Chester Stern when I was bowling. Trying to clutch a belted return catch, the ball shot off my palm and hit the stumps with Chester out of his ground, backing up. It was unintentional and I was suitably apologetic whenever I had to sort out his computer after that.

Sports desk had annual golf outings to Royal West Norfolk, near Hunstanton. We'd go up on the Sunday night, play a round in the morning before a convivial lunch and then play another round before heading home. In April 1996, we were on a jolly that coincided with the last round of the US Masters.

Our host, Adrian Brown, whose son Oliver is a sportswriter, persuaded the publican of his local, the Lifeboat Inn at Thornham, to bring a TV to the snug and we watched transfixed as Nick Faldo overcame a six-shot deficit to Greg Norman to win his third Masters.

We were genuinely shocked as the Aussie played a succession of duff shots not unfamiliar to us all. It tied the largest lead blown in a PGA Tour tournament – a record that still stands. Faldo shot 67 and Norman 78. More famous capitulation that epic victory.

Norman clearly got a little ahead of himself, as have I at this point. Although my association with the MoS was longer, my first full-time Fleet Street job took me to the races.

14 This Sporting Life

For a good few years, I had earned a decent living by doing shifts at more than one place. It was nomadic and not unusual – and a great way to raise your profile as you awaited your first proper full-time gig. In one week I might work at The Times, The Mail on Sunday and The Sporting Life, my regular haunts.

Sometimes I would do two shifts in a day... five hours at the MoS on a Thursday or Friday morning, setting up the weekend's results coverage and checking league tables had been updated, before walking up to Holborn Circus to work at the Life.

That would save me a train fare and buy a day off – but it came with some drawbacks: no holiday or sick pay, and you felt duty-bound to accept all the shifts put your way in case you didn't get asked back.

The Times, which was then in Grays Inn Road, was a venerable institution – and that came through even on the sports desk, which had a ritualised 4pm tea round. We would take it in turns to fill the big old urn and wash the cups.

It felt like an anachronistic hangover from a bygone age, but nonetheless, it was quaint and a chance to stop work and chat. But we seldom saw any execs from other departments venture across – we were very much an island and didn't overly mind that. I actually missed those cuppas when, during the 1980 Moscow Olympics, I worked at The Times through the night, compiling all the results from the Games, down to the also-rans, in every sport, ready to hand over in the morning.

The Times was by far the least boisterous of the three papers to work at; the sports subs were parked on one long desk and you were more likely to discuss obscure footballers of the 1950s (it helped that former England captain Billy Wright's son, Vince, worked with us) than the latest scrape a current 'star' had gotten into.

Nick Harling ran The Times football team and had the distinction of being the craziest driver I have known. He'd give us a lift back to the office after matches and it was not unknown for him to go up pavements or dip the wrong way down one-way streets to get us back on time for our shift. Highway Code? What's that? Traffic cameras today would have reined in his excesses at the wheel – and yet I never felt scared when he was on one. Perhaps I should have done.

One year we got to the Fleet Street League cup final, which was played at Selhurst Park. I remember coming out of the Crystal Palace FC tunnel and thinking, "this pitch isn't very long". But, boy, was it wide.

I had an overhead kick which hit both the bar then the post before running to safety, which a staff photographer managed to capture, and we lost 3-2 to the Express. But it was an experience to play on such a ground, the home of Palace and also, for a time, Wimbledon – two First Division clubs. Players of today would not recognise the place: the dressing-rooms were no bigger or better kept than some I'd used in park pavilions, though they had a big communal bath rather than showers.

We got on great with most of our opponents, especially The Guardian, whose team was run by football writer Phil Shaw. They were short-handed for a newspaper tournament in Amsterdam one time and I guested for them, sending the keeper the wrong way in a penalty shootout as we lifted the trophy. It did feel a bit odd to be invited to an event, then going home with the hosts' silver. Cue conversation at Customs: "Anything to declare, lads?"

"Just this silver thing." Victory in Europe tasted

sweet, that's for sure.

The following midweek I helped organise a friendly for a scratch Life team against The Times and turned out for the Life. Having just played several matches at the weekend, I had never felt so fit, scoring a hat-trick. I felt I could have played another game that day though it was a downhill trot from there!

The staff job at The Sporting Life came out of the blue, after I had been working there three or four times a week. The Life was hugely respected among a niche readership – though not as exclusive as its owner Robert Maxwell once might have thought, mistakenly calling it Country Life. It was, uniquely, the arbiter of betting disputes between bookmakers and punters. It stood up for punters' rights.

It was also the Queen Mother's favourite paper, which she let slip in a TV interview. Our editor at the time, Monty Court, was not slow in picking up on that, getting T-shirts printed with the elderly royal's quote: "Of course I read The Sporting Life."

It was totally unlike any other paper in that it had to be designed to be pinned up on betting shop walls. The bookies didn't want to buy lots of copies for each shop, so you had to make sure the card and form for one race meeting did not appear back-to back. I am so glad I didn't have to plan that.

We had some incredibly colourful characters, the most oddball, by more than a short-head, being John McCririck. He was the deerstalker and cape-wearing pundit known to TV viewers for his arm-waving theatrics. He worked mostly on the racecourse and I only saw him in the office a couple of times, always with his wife, the long-suffering Jennifer, whom he called, somewhat disparagingly, though he would say endearingly, "The Booby". She would fall into step the requisite distance behind him as he marched in to see the boss. Among her many and varied services on his behalf was to be his chauffeur, because the Old Harrovian couldn't drive.

TV critic Nina Myskow once described McCririck as having "all the charm of an armpit". He was a caricature of himself but a very good campaigning journalist, who won two British Press awards, including Racing Journalist of the Year in 1979 after exposing a series of betting frauds at the Tote, the on-course betting organisation.

An unrelenting series of exposes with help from Tote insiders led Mac to round on its chief, Woodrow Wyatt, who also happened to be a fellow Mirror Group employee, as a long-time columnist. But John was never able to land the final blow, with Prime Minister Maggie Thatcher and Home Secretary Willie Whitelaw appearing in Wyatt's corner. He was ennobled as Lord Wyatt of Weeford but his reputation within racing circles was shredded by the stories McCririck produced.

McCririck was sacked by the Life in 1984 – the year he successfully sued the Daily Star following allegations that he was in debt to an on-course bookmaker. The office grapevine claimed he had been bailed out financially at least once by the paper, and threatened by another rails bookmaker that he might become a central tunnel support on the new M25 if he didn't pay up what he owed. He indeed admitted owing money – but said he had been placing bets for others.

His own star continued on its rise after that case, albeit on TV. While even his closest friends recognised McCririck's many shortcomings, there was another side to him. Underneath that bizarely eccentric exterior was an insecure, sometimes generous man.

Former Lifer Mike Cattermole said: "Not many people know that when John appeared on Big Brother, quite a sizeable portion of his fee went to charity. He made a song and dance about a lot of things but never the fact that he was a great supporter of many racing charities. He had an extremely generous heart."

My time at the paper coincided with the end of Ossie Fletcher's 26-year reign as editor. It was poor Graham Taylor who had to deal with constant interruptions to print runs, McCririck's final indiscretions, the occasional legal issue – plus he 11pm calls at home from Maxwell. Cap'n Bob, as he was dubbed, would have been at some function or other with someone he saw as influential. They had a racing-related bit of gossip and he wanted it in the paper the next day – with no thought, understanding or interest that the paper had already gone to press. Graham, in the end, was happy to get out of

Dodge with his pension intact and bought his company car for £1 by all accounts.

Chief sub Noel Blunt was a legend in his own break time. "Noool – Blunt by name, Blunt by nature," colleagues such as Alan Smith and Brummie Bryan Pugh would say. A say-it-like-it-is Yorkshireman with a love of France, where he had a holiday home in the Dordogne, Blunty was a latter-day Mrs Malaprop.

"We'll cross that bridge when it arrives" was one of his classic sayings. And he must have been proud of it as he said it more than once to my certain knowledge.

"The hanging baskets of Babylon" was another. As was his declaration: "Those blooming football hooligans – if I had my way, I'd shove them on a desolate island and throw away the key."

He wrote a much scoffed at headline about a particular horse "scaling the Eider" – mixing the Eider Chase, run in Newcastle, with the Eiger mountain in Switzerland. You could not put him right.

One of our best photographers was Irishman Ed Byrne, who happened, for his day job, to be a London bus conductor. Handily, his route went past the Mirror building, enabling him to drop off his prints from the weekend.

I worked on the features desk, led by the brilliant Alastair Down, with John Watson, who had a welcome habit of always being able to lift the mood when the going got dull. Dear Johnny – or 'Hen' as we nicknamed him because of his middle name, Henry

– did a very passable Maxwell impression and was seeing our pages away in the print room one evening when he trotted it out for the comps, not realising Maxwell was actually standing behind him. Johnny thankfully still had a job the next day. Maxwell was most likely flattered by the imitation.

John also recounted how Eve Pollard, then editor of the Sunday Mirror, had been out for a heavy lunch when she wandered into the print room to see how her pages were coming together. She was loudly and rudely critical of a number of them – only to be told gently by a comp that they were actually the Sunday People pages and hers were over the other side of the room.

Alastair and Monty Court liked my page designs – I knew nothing about racing – and they gave me free rein. A couple of them were framed and sent to the British Horseracing Museum in Newmarket, though I have never been to see if they are on display or just gathering dust in a forgotten cupboard.

Monty was a great Fleet Street character. As a reporter, he was once sent to cover a round-the-world yachtsman, I think it was Alec Rose, and file a daily diary. He told his boss: "I could write that now... Day 1: sailed all day, saw fuck all. Day 2: Ditto."

He was one of the most approachable bosses I have known and was often in our features department for a natter. He did knock back one of my cheekiest headlines, though. A rider named John Deutsch won this particular point-to-point race in emphatic style and I floated the line: "Deutsch Lands Master

Race". I was chuffed with it, though of course I realised it might not be politically correct. It got binned, sadly.

Alastair organised a memorable Christmas lunch for us one year – in April. The festive period was always a very busy time on the Life as there is a huge Boxing Day racing programme, culminating with the King George Chase at Kempton – one of the steeplechasing year's highlights. December was so busy with features, some for advance pages so we could get a bit of the festive period off. So, April it was, and we had a brilliant Chinese meal (the staff even got into the spirit, donning Santa hats and providing Christmas crackers) followed by an afternoon's racing at Sandown.

Al, who majored in the sport at public school, had a great, self-deprecating sense of humour and would say he had "a face fit for radio" – but he became a regular and engaging racing presenter on Channel 4 TV. Cheltenham was the unrivalled highlight of the year for a man who idolised jump racing and derided the Flat as "ferret racing".

The Life was awash with fantastic nicknames. I am not sure that I had been bestowed with such an honour, though I did have my own song, courtesy of Mike Weinstein, along-time Evening Standard sports guy who shifted on the MoS. He'd go: 'You're Paul Fry, Fry, hush hush, aye doo aye,' to the tune of a Kajagoogoo hit. My love of golf also earned me the epithet Fryesteros, after the great Spaniard, Seve Ballesteros.

The Sporting Life had Rigsby, after the Leonard Rossiter character (Jeff Ballard); Winkle (Colin McKie); Poid (Kevin Impey); Benny the Wad (Brian Clements); Plum (Geoff Duffield); The Admiral (John Benbow); Hopper (Paul Duffett); Scouse (Andy Harrison); Jock – but never to his face – (Bob Halestrap); Shagger (Gary Nutting); Scarlett (John O'Hara); Bobby The Toe (Bob Toseland); Eddie the Shoe (Eddie Fremantle); and The Bishop (John Santer, whose brother was a real bishop). All we were missing were Dirtbox and Chinese Alan for the full Smithy from Gavin and Stacey set.

The tipsters used a language all their own and Dave Cox – Coxy – a gentle giant who journeyed in each day from Swaffham, in the Fens, was one of the best. Geoff Lester was top man in the field, an excellent writer. Alastair had a gift for spotting talent and brought in columnists with their fingers on the pulse all over the country, from Ireland, the US and Far East, with expertise from bloodstock and breeding to tips from the gallops on which stables were hot and those that were not.

Jamie Lambie was a quietly-spoken, highly knowledgeable figure based in the North and wrote a fascinatingly forensic history of the paper, The Story of Your Life, which detailed the Life's many ups and downs from 1859 until its demise in 1998. It is as much a work of racing history as the paper was.

The Life had a boxing correspondent, Malcolm Hanover, a likeable a guy who shared my support for Tottenham Hotspur and, of course, boxing. He would go to the big fights in London when he could, and to West End cinemas when big bouts in the States were beamed back live in the small hours. The rest of us would only get to see the fight in full on TV the next evening.

Malcolm had this peculiar nervous affliction, where he'd grip his tie and throw his head round in a circle and then backwards while still holding on to his tie and would end up momentarily looking skyward.

One day in April 1985, Malcolm had gone his whole shift waiting to see the hotly-anticipated Thomas Hearns v Marvin Hagler world middle-weight title showdown on delayed transmission. It had happened in the early hours our time in Para-dise, near Las Vegas. "Don't tell me the result, don't tell me the result," he begged us all day. "I want to watch it when I get in, as if it was live."

He put his coat on to head home, having studi-ously avoided all word of the fight, which was quite an achievement in a newspaper office. That's when his trademark tic kicked in – round and back went his head. Some bugger had stuck a piece of paper to the ceiling with "Hagler in the third", emblazoned on it in capitals. Know your audience, they say.

Sad to say Malcolm, the last of three bachelor brothers who shared a flat off the Edgware Road, died just as I was finishing this book, following a broken hip and complications amid a brief stay in hospital.

As Paul Duffett said: "It was somehow fitting that

his beloved Spurs were top of the Premier League as he left the stage for the last time."

Mick 'Molly' Malone, another former Lifer, said of Malcolm: "He had a very dry sense of humour. He backed Germany to win the 1990 World Cup and stood to win a substantial amount, and said: "I must be the only Jewish bloke that wants the Germans to win."

And I didn't realise until recently that the former music hall comic entertainer, Bud Flanagan, of Flanagan and Allen, was a close family friend of Malcolm.

The lads were always up for a stunt at someone's expense – once it involved someone doing a fake phone commentary of a race from the back of the room, complete with a bit of background hiss and timely interjections such as: "They're just going behind at Kelso..." for a layer of added authenticity.

There followed a brilliant, unscripted commentary for the unsuspecting listener, Jeff Ballard, whose job as "stick-up man" was to prepare the racing results as they came off the paper agency feeds. He was tricked this time into believing his daily and much-lampooned 10p yankee had come up.

Moments later, the real result then appeared on the agency ticker – for Jeff, seeing the result in black and white, the reality dawned of yet another accumulator going down the drain, his anticipated windfall already "spent" in his mind, no doubt.

Jeremy Chapman was one of the page planners, with Ernie – the fastest page man in the West –

Dymock. Jeremy doubled up as golf correspondent. Like a small number of Lifers, he used his knowledge of both his chosen sport and betting odds to advise the bookies (for a small but regular fee), ensuring they didn't get caught with their pants down by offering too generous a price on players in various events. His wife was German and they once had a little-known German golfer, new to the European Tour, as a lodger. It was Bernhard Langer – later to become a European Tour regular, a Ryder Cup star and US Masters winner.

Jeremy arranged a brilliant farewell gift for me when I moved to the MoS – a press ticket to go with him to the Ryder Cup at The Belfry. We were there throughout the four days – for practice and the three days' competition, staying over at a hotel nearby – and Jeremy's punting nous helped us more than cover some of my expenses. He doubtless claimed his own!

With our badges, we were able to follow the action from inside the ropes and I was crouched behind Nick Faldo as he holed out from a deep, greenside bunker at one short hole to fire up the already noisily enthusiastic home fans.

This was September 1989 and one of my personal highlights was seeing Seve Ballesteros, who ignited the Ryder Cup when it was in the doldrums, helping to win the event a global audience.

It is surprising now to think this was the first Ryder Cup to be shown live on TV in the US. It ended in a 14-14 tie, but with Europe being the holders, they retained the trophy and showered a hugely boisterous crowd with bubbly from the roof of The Belfry Hotel.

JC later got 'put out to grass', as he described it, by the Racing Post. He was great company on that Birmingham trip and the golf was just a joy.

The Life was owned by Maxwell's Mirror Group and you'd take a signed timesheet up to the ninth floor of the Mirror building, across a covered bridge from Orbit House where we were based, to get paid in cash each week. One night, I was standing behind an in-house electrician and the cashier was counting out a huge pile of £20s for him. It was a veritable cashcade. I opined meekly that I was only collecting about £140, so could they kindly save a few notes for me! On my first shift, I was in the Mirror canteen for a meal break when a guy approached me and said: "You're about the right size. Here, come with me..." He led me to his locker, in a small room off a nearby corridor and offered me this smart, new shiny grey suit for £35. I think it was made in Bulgaria or somewhere in Eastern Europe, but I bought one as I was not over-endowed with suits. His locker was an Aladdin's cave, full of perfumes, aftershaves and watches – there were more dodgy tickers there than in a care home.

This is when I learned that most of the printers had their little "sidelines". Some had market stalls up the road in Leather Lane. They would clock in, go straight out to work a few hours on their stall, then come back later to do a bit of toil before clocking off. Some had other gigs. One lunchtime I was playing football for The Times against the Express at Southwark Park. There was a row of at least half a dozen black cabs parked in a tidy row when we arrived. I innocently asked one of my team-mates if the cabbies' team were playing on the next pitch to us – but they were all Express comps: compositors, or typesetters, and other print staff that we called 'Inkeys'.

The joke was that these guys were so well off they were like the Incas, only from southern Spain, near the villas which many of them owned. There, on the Costas, you'd find the Lost City of the Inkeys. And, like those Incas from Mexico, their time would one day come to an end.

These guys were mostly EastEnders who had used their piles cash to move out to bigger piles in Essex. Many played golf and had perma-tans from a combination of the wife's sunbed and multiple holidays abroad each year. And they weren't shy in bragging about it.

They had all this because of the stranglehold the print unions held over managements in Fleet Street. They had the muscle to halt production if the bosses tried to rein them in.

There were pay scams – 'Spanish practices', as Robert Maxwell termed them – such as actually inventing employees and sharing the pay around, perhaps while taunting management by using made-up names such as 'D Duck' or 'M Mouse'. It was a closed shop: you had to know someone or be related to someone to get a job 'in the print'. If you did, you were seemingly set for life.

There was a lot of banter between the Inkeys and those of us who worked the 'stone', where the pages were assembled, and we would check them for errors, mark cuts to get overly-long stories to fit, or bump things out if they fell a bit short, then proofread the pages before sending them off to print. Word was, at some sites, that one shift of typesetters would deliberately make mistakes so the next shift would be needed to correct them.

The Inkeys were fiercely protective of their jobs, the more so as the end loomed large, though I suspect many were still in denial until the last, such was the powerful sway they held. They were especially grumpy during the days of paste-up, when stories came out on photographic paper and had to be cut, waxed then stuck to layout boards. Woe betide any stone sub who, without thinking, pointed out something that needed doing by touching the boards. These guys wielded very sharp scalpels.

But there was a storm coming. A violent one.

15 Everyone Out

The 1980s changed Fleet Street forever. Many other industries too, of course, irrevocably. No longer were managements prepared to be held to ransom by the print unions. Rupert Murdoch took them on by moving the Sun and The Times to Wapping, in east London, without the printers, and won a long, bitter dispute.

After the near year-long miners' strike of 1984-85, the 54-week Wapping dispute was a second major defeat for the unions – and a victory for Prime Minister Margaret Thatcher that echoes loudly even today.

Wapping was marked by a series of violent clashes between police and print workers and, judging by a Radio 4 programme, The Reunion, which brought together some of the key protagonists to discuss the matter, a raw and very deep bitterness is still there – on both sides. Listening back again, I sensed the union rep would have been quite happy to have been left alone in a room with former Sun editor Kelvin McKenzie so they could revisit the "good old days".

The dispute broke the newspaper print workers' unions and emboldened the Government and many other industries to redress years of imbalance in power between companies and unions. You could, of course, argue that, with the rise of zero-hours contracts and the loss of hard-won working rights, things have now swung too far in the opposite direction.

Even journalists, who had for a long time benefited by going in with their pay claims on the tail-coats of the printers, would never have it so good again.

Individual contracts ended collective bargaining deals and there was a gradual driving down of pay rates. Often a new employee would be on much less than the person they replaced – and with none of the former's benefits, such as private health cover or a company car.

Generous expenses allowances started to disappear. The days of blagging blank taxi receipts from a friendly cabbie in return for a decent tip were numbered. Whoever said there's no such thing as a free lunch was wise indeed – and ahead of his or her time.

Britain's national newspapers began to open new plants and abandon their Fleet Street homes, adopting technology that required far fewer employees. No wonder the press barons were grateful to Thatcher, as their hated industrial landscape was brutally bulldozed and refashioned more to their liking.

It was a time of enormous social strife, including the Poll Tax, which Thatcher instigated in 1989 and led to riots – even the imprisoning of a Liverpool Labour MP, Terry Fields, for refusing to pay the Community Charge, as it was officially called.

I went on strike only once – the National Union of Journalists' (NUJ) stoppage lasted just over six weeks, from December 5, 1978, until January 17, 1979, though a group of journos at the Nottingham Evening Post stayed out for three years. It started at the Post, then run by Post owners T Bailey Foreman, over union demands for a £20 pay rise across the board when the Government was trying to hold pay rises to below 5pc.

If you think that sounds demanding, UK inflation was running at 8.5pc in 1978 and spiralled to more than 13pc the following year. That meant £1 in 1978 had the same buying power as £1.13 a year later. Interest rates which soared to 17.5pc meant crippling mortgage payments for many people and plummeting living standards.

Inflation and industrial strife led in part to Maggie Thatcher's rise to power in May 1979 - the year when Sid Vicious of the Sex Pistols was found dead in his New York hotel, Trevor Francis became football's first £1m player, Lord Mountbatten was murdered by the IRA and a naturist beach opened in Brighton.

I was working in Uxbridge, at the Slough and Hounslow Evening Mail and living away from my Stevenage home for the first time. I did a few stints on that freezing picket line outside the plant in Cricketfield Road (Picketfield Road, as we renamed it), where we could see management upstairs, included the hated Acton Gazette editor, Alan Prosser, get staff photographers to capture images of us all. We had little if any strike pay, and I had no choice, to pay my bills, other than to find some casual work through a temping agency.

I did a couple of weeks with Neff, moving fridges and ovens. The washing machines with lumps of concrete in them nearly did for me. Then I got a couple of weeks at Heathrow Airport in a department where they updated the pilots' manuals with details of new landmarks or beacons on flight routes. I kept an anxious watch on the news for a while after that, in case I had made a mistake and caused a crash somewhere! Lunch hours were spent wandering around the departure check-in areas, imagining I was jetting off somewhere exotic, or on the observation deck just taking in the seeming chaos.

The agency then got me a gig as a secretary at the

fruit juice firm, Kia-Ora, typing staff menus and the odd letter for an initially confused boss, an Aussie ("they sent me a blohke?!"). He was good company and used to let me go early, have long lunches and was sympathetic to our union's cause when I explained my predicament.

Money was tight, even as deputy sports editor at the Evening Mail. It was always handy when I had a home Brentford game to cover and the visiting team's local paper didn't send anyone, as I would get some orders for words from them - sometimes I'd do two or even three reports on the same game, often phoned over in chunks during the game and on the final whistle.

The Evening Mail editor, the gruff, moustachioed Chris Fowler, was an inspiring figure who had come from the Southend Evening Echo, where he had won awards. His office wall had an old Echo front page from when the pier went up in flames. He actually quite hated the "editor" part of his job, with all its attendant paperwork, and was never happier than when he was out on the subs' desk, sleeves rolled up, working his magic on mundane stories.

The sports editor, Brian Sansome, was from Reading and loved his weekend getaways with the wife to their caravan at Hayling Island. He told this great tale against himself about how, when he was with the Reading Post, he was designing their Saturday night football edition – a fast-turnaround job intended to catch fans almost straight after the match finished.

"I'd drawn up this brilliant front page, and it was getting late when someone asked where all the results and league tables (which always went on the front) were to go." It was a real Homer Simpson-esque 'Doh' moment.

I was renting rooms in a place on the Hayes-Southall border with a mate, Paul Hazard, also from Stevenage, who had a chef's job in Harrow. I found it amusing that, as I got the 207 bus through the area to and from work in Uxbridge, the only non-Asian shop I'd see was Currys.

The morning bus ride of about an hour to Uxbridge did have one bonus: if it was on time, I'd be treated to the sight of Concorde on the apron or taxiway – or actually taking off, on a runway parallel to our route. What a sight that was. Such an elegant beast. And such a cross-Channel collaboration.

As impoverished as I was, I dated a trainee reporter who, it turned out, was the daughter of the Westminster Press newspaper group's chairman, Sir Frank Barlow. She lived in some fancy pile out in Gerrards Cross, in leafy Buckinghamshire though I didn't get the invite home.

Neither did Kim visit my Southall bedsit but she drove – I couldn't afford to run a car – and was bright, engaging and very attractive. However, I felt awkward and inadequate when she insisted on paying for dinner at an Uxbridge restaurant. I felt she was out of my league, that I might go down with her parents like a lead balloon. Much as she had an obvious liking for me – she must have, she even went with me to cover a football match at the glorious venue that was Feltham Arena. Unlike the steady stream of planes constantly flying overhead, it didn't go anywhere between us.

I did much better financially once I started working in Fleet Street, never more so than when I joined The Sporting Life full time in 1985. We got seven weeks' holiday a year – and generous expenses, including being able to claim for your TV rental (yes, rental) and a full set of the papers each day, when you may have bought only a couple of them.

There was also a weekly 'racing allowance'. I seldom went to a racecourse but was still able to claim it. It would be letting the side down if I did not. Usually, it just involved working out where there was a Midlands race meeting that would take you me to the required weekly allowance in rail fare and sticking that down on a claim form. I went to Warwick quite a lot, as far as the pay office were concerned. I have been past the racecourse there a few times in latter years, it is not far from the Castle, but never to a meeting. Receipts? Who needed them?

After five years, you qualified for an extra four weeks off as a sabbatical. I didn't quite get there but I have no regrets about my first staff job in town.

And it was during my time at the Life that I had a brush with disaster – when I got caught up in a football stadium tragedy in Belgium in which 39 people were killed just a few yards of where I had been standing on th Heysel Stadium terraces.

16 *Heysel*

It is a memory that is impossible to erase and never dulls: rows of bodies, covered loosely with flags and arranged in haphazard fashion on the ground outside a football stadium. There was no dignity in death, either, as the downdraft from emergency helicopters disturbed the giant banners, leaving the victims exposed amid the confusion and mayhem at Brussels' Heysel Stadium.

Some 50,000 tickets had been sold for the 1985 European Cup final. When the day was done, 39 people were dead, all of whom perished within just a few yards of where I had been standing on terraces that were left to resemble a war zone. These poor people, mostly Italians, had been trampled and suffocated when a stadium wall collapsed as they had tried to avoid a hail of missiles thrown by Liverpool fans in the next pen.

In the cold light of the next day, as the quest for answers – and justice – began, we were presented with a scene comprising lumps of concrete, bent and toppled crush-barriers, the collapsed pitch-side wall – and all manner of discarded clothing, scarves and even the occasional match programme or ticket.

I had chills that morning when I realised how close I had come to being more seriously ensnared in what happened – and more so when I read for the first time only recently the story of one man from Northern Ireland who was among the dead. It was largely assumed the dead had been solely Italians.

Patrick Radcliffe, 39, from Belfast, worked as an archivist for the EEC (the forerunner to the EU) in Brussels and didn't even like football. He was on a night out with a friend who had a spare match ticket. But he never went home. Patrick's twin, George, said of him: "He was in the wrong place at the wrong time". Patrick and too many others.

Heysel foreshadowed an even greater tragedy, at Hillsborough, in Sheffield, four years later. There were more victims then – 96 – and the carnage then was followed by a 30-year quest for justice.

I was in the city to visit a Belgian girlfriend, An, and, on the off-chance, went to the stadium on the morning of the game, between Liverpool, the defending European champions, and the Italian team Juventus. I was surprised to see only a short line at a small hut that served as a makeshift ticket office and had no problems in getting one, I think for the Belgian Francs equivalent of about £15. I was excited at the prospect of seeing a major sports event. The diehard supporters of both clubs had their tickets already and the ones sold on matchday were meant for 'neutrals' in a large section, Block Z – one of three equally-sized segments behind one goal. This would become significant later.

Mission accomplished, I went back to the capital's beautiful medieval central square, the Grand Place. It was a bright, hot, end of May day and there was a bustling flower market on the cobbles of the huge main square, which is surrounded by quaint stone and timbered buildings that serve as restaurants and cafes.

To one side, a newly-married couple emerged blinking in strong sunlight from the old town hall. They were immediately serenaded by fans of both Liverpool and Juventus. For now, at least, there was harmony. But the discord was not long in coming.

As a broiling day wore on, it was evident that a good many Italian fans were content to repair to a cafe for a meal washed down by a glass or two of wine. For all too many red-shirted Liverpool supporters, their menu selection was a shopping trolley filled with dumpy beer bottles from a supermarket down a side street near the Mannekin Pis statue.

The mood visibly darkened as the drinks went

down. In late afternoon, police cordoned off a street where a jeweller's shop had had its windows stoved in, with some items reportedly stolen. And yet I went on the Metro to the stadium believing that things were merely the scally side of boisterous and no more.

Twice in fairly recent history, Englishmen arriving in Belgium had been a welcome sight – armed as they were with proper weaponry, deployed against the Germans. This "English army" was stripped to the waist and tooled up only with alcohol.

I got to the ground early and was immediately mystified as to why the Juventus fans at the far end were occupying all three sections behind the opposite goal, while the Liverpool contingent were to be shoehorned into just the two to my left. It was early but the red section was already looking pretty full. Surely, I wondered, it would be obvious that many more fans would travel the shorter distance from Merseyside than from Turin.

Block Z was, by comparison, comfortably roomy. I was standing to the rear and left of the pen, as I faced the pitch, close to the chain-link fence separating us from the Liverpool fans. There was barely anyone in front of me, all the way to the front wall, which was not a formidable structure by any means. Even I would have been able to scale it. Once hostilities began, I did at one point briefly go to the front, thinking that might be safer, with an exit onto the pitch, before retreating, realising that all the realistic exits were behind me.

It is my honest belief that things began to turn ugly when the Liverpool fans noticed that the vast majority in Z Block were Italian. They were embedded locals or expats taking advantage of the chance to see a team from their homeland in a major final right on their doorstep. The hotheads in the Liverpool pen became ever more agitated as they felt increasingly overcrowded and their aggression was aimed towards these Italian fans.

Disturbances in grounds were typical of the time: a series of thuggish outbursts in England had made football such an unedifying sight that the TV companies were not queueing to put the game on the nation's screens and money into the football authorities' coffers. Indeed, with the most recent TV contract having elapsed there would be no new deal, and thus no football on UK screens, until early 1986 – and that after a deal for just £1.3million. That wouldn't buy Harry Kane's left big toenail.

Missiles – lumps of the terracing that crumbled away easily with a well-aimed kick of the heel – started to rain down, all well over my head. Those to my right, trying to evade the barrage, huddled together and shielded their heads with their forearms as far away as possible. That is when a pitch-side wall gave way and people were squashed and trampled.

There were despairing images of people, mostly men, with their arms outstretched pleading for help. But first-aid assistance was slow. I saw fans use metal rail barriers and advertising hoardings as makeshift stretchers. One poor chap was carried away on railings, his large form covered with a Juventus flag, and I was jolted at the sight of his arm then falling loose and hanging down limply from the railing.

For a couple of years, I had been working shifts with The Times sports desk and The Mail on Sunday and felt, with a major story breaking around me, that I should try to see if I could get into the press box to describe to sportswriters I knew what I had seen. I had a unique perspective, being right among it all. While you don't seek to be the focus of a story, I figured it might look odd if I mentioned only days later that I had been there and had said nothing. The press box would also offer some sanctuary from the violence, with the Liverpool fans now clawing at the fence to try to gain access into Z Block.

I started to make my way out past a couple of disinterested policemen at the back and saw, to my right, holes that had been pushed or kicked through the breeze-block outer skin of the stadium, allowing access for anyone without a ticket. I had met some ticketless fans on the ferry from Dover and on the train from Ostend, including one whose rail ticket was for the trip from Liverpool to Bootle, but it had the word 'Bootle' crossed out and 'Belgium' scribbled on instead. He couldn't spell Brussels, he said, and didn't have a ticket for the game; he would take his chances.

The scene that greeted me outside the ground was like something from a Bruce Willis movie set:

there were police, ambulances, random uniformed people walking about and helicopters overhead, shining down spotlights. At the main entrance, staff on the reception were busy and distracted, so I followed the signs up the stairs to the press box, which I entered, unchallenged.

As I started chatting to one reporter I knew, I was overheard by a BBC Radio producer and he asked if I would do an interview. Next thing, I was sitting beside the former Liverpool captain, Emlyn Hughes, who was in tears as I recounted the happy wedding scenes and the descent into madness and death. This was his club, he wore his beating red heart on his sleeve. Its reputation was being shredded before his reddening eyes.

I didn't know until I got back home to Stevenage that my mum had heard the interview, which had been used on TV news, and so she knew I was safe. She knew that I was in the city but not whether I had gone to the game.

I could now see that the chain-link fence I had stood beside had been torn down and Liverpool fans had poured through into Z Block. There was a cloud of tear-gas, and police with riot shields were engaged in running battles with Liverpool fans. In all, 600 people were injured that night.

For an hour, they fought to quell the violence and pulled bodies from the rubble. Around me, I could hear a debate about whether the game could, or should, go ahead. There were divisions in opinion. From a public order point of view, as the rioting raged, there was no alternative but for the match to go ahead. It would buy the police time to put in place a post-game strategy and avoid more bloodshed in wider Brussels; it was best contained.

But the players did not want to play. Word reached us that their spouses and partners, in the stadium for what should have been a showpiece occasion, were distraught. Kenny Dalglish's wife, Marina, was later quoted as saying that she had prayed he didn't get a penalty as she feared for him if he had scored.

As it was, Michel Platini did score from the penalty spot – right in front of the Liverpool fans. Juventus won the match 1-0 and the trophy but the game itself, especially in England, was the loser.

You could argue that Heysel was inevitable. There had been a dangerous cocktail hidden in plain sight: key people in authority had foreseen it happening. There had even been warnings from Liverpool FC. But the match organisers, UEFA, did nothing. Putting aside the stadium concerns, there had been a fear for Liverpool fans' safety following the Liverpool-Roma final in Rome a year earlier when there was a lot of violence aimed their way. It was feared some of the Liverpool contingent might come looking for revenge, ignoring the fact Roma were not in the final and that any Italian would do. That was the mentality of a small but worryingly destructive minority, I would say, hell-bent on havoc.

The stadium was of 1920s construction and not fit for purpose. The ticketing arrangements were an invitation for trouble. The owners of Heysel, the Bel-

gian police and UEFA were all investigated for culp-
ability. Albert Roosens, head of the Belgian Football
Association, was tried for allowing tickets for Block
Z to be sold to Juventus fans. Captain Johan Mahieu,
the police officer who was responsible for Z Block,
was given a nine-month suspended sentence. Roosens was handed a six-month suspended jail term.

In a separate civil action brought by family members, four officials were found not liable for the
deaths that resulted from the tragedy. They included Jacques Georges, the former president of
UEFA; Hans Bangerter, former UEFA general secretary; former Brussels Mayor Herve Brouhon; and
Viviane Baro, a former Brussels councillor for
sports.

But after an 18-month investigation, Belgian judge
Marina Coppieters concluded that blame should
rest solely with the Liverpool fans. In fact 24 Liverpool fans were extradited on involuntary man-
slaughter charges, with 14 found guilty, following
a trial, on April 28, 1989, almost four years after
the tragedy – it was a lengthy legal process. Those
fans found guilty were sentenced to three years in
prison, 18 months of which was suspended. Some
might say those convicted didn't serve enough
time, but that's a different argument.

Reds' fan Peter Hooton, lead singer of The Farm,
a former youth worker, was at the game and said
the venue was totally unsuitable but that "you just
thought six Merseyside police officers with experience of Anfield and Goodison would have sorted out

what was happening in two minutes".

"The police, or security, seemed to react by attacking, and things escalated to a point of no return."

Hooliganism had for too long been an embarrassing stain on English football and, the day after Heysel, Prime Minister Margaret Thatcher started a process that would lead to its clubs being banned from European competition for five years – Liverpool for an additional year.

The Anfield club qualified for Europe competition in five of those six years, three as League champions. Other clubs such as Derby County and even Liverpool's city rivals Everton, were also excluded – and this in an era when English clubs had been the dominant force in European competition.

All-seater stadia, CCTV, better policing and banning orders have helped hugely in curtailing violence in football grounds. Known troublemakers are kept from travelling abroad, though there have still been major incidents involving England fans, notably in Italy in 1990 and at the Euros in Portugal in 2004. Heysel was rebuilt after the tragedy but there are plans for a new Tottenham-style super-stadium to take its place.

The sad postscript is the part Heysel played in what happened at Hillsborough. Police and football officials were conditioned by events at Heysel and other stadia, believing that stadium disturbances were always the direct result of hooliganism.

Thus, when 96 fans died in Sheffield, crushed

against the fences and on the terraces at the FA Cup semi-final between Liverpool and Nottingham Forest, the first instinct of those in charge was to blame hooliganism. But it wasn't the cause at all – and that stubborn insistence, and refusal to accept the fact, stopped the families of those who died from getting justice, and even due process, for more than two decades.

Those Liverpool fans, including sisters and young children, died through poor crowd management, and yet the police deflected blame on their part by spinning – even repeating in court – that the Liverpool fans were to blame in Sheffield. It was a narrative that was fed in the immediate aftermath to compliant sections of the media, notably the Sun. But it found a wider traction.

The families' fight is still not over; their cause far from fully satisfied by having those they see as being culpable judged and punished properly for their actions that day.

The tale of Heysel is retold every anniversary, and that is a good thing. Lessons were undoubtedly learned. Stadia facilities and the way fans are treated have improved beyond all recognition, as have policing and match-day organisation. England has enough top-notch stadia to host a World Cup at short notice.

And, while the Premier League is a money pit limply disguised as a fair competition, we must hope that never again will fans spend an afternoon or evening at a football match, never to return home.

17 Tragedy and mystery

I t was early evening and I was heading home from the Sporting Life, whose offices were then in Farringdon Road. There was a strong smell of smoke as I waited for a Tube train at Farringdon back to King's Cross, to get my connection to Stevenage. But all local Underground services had been halted, with no explanation other than that they could be out for quite a while, so I began the walk, which took about 25 minutes.

This was November 18, 1987 – the night of the fire at King's Cross that killed 31 people and injured 100. The blaze had broken out at about the time I left the office, and was caused by a match discarded on a wooden escalator to the Piccadilly Line and which set light to piles of litter in the void below.

Fire Brigade station officer Colin Townsley, in charge of the first pump fire engine to arrive, was in the main ticket hall when there was a flashover. He was killed. His body was found beside that of a badly-burnt passenger at the exit steps to Pancras Road. It is believed he had seen her in difficulty and stopped to help. He was posthumously awarded the George Medal.

Smoking on the London Underground had been banned in July 1984, yet this tragedy was caused by a match. Looking back, it is astonishing to re-call now just how prevalent smoking was in public spaces. I had a really nice suit (not the Bulgarian one from my days on the Life) that was damaged by someone's cigarette while I was queuing at the bar in a pub – proof that drinking and smoking really are bad for you.

We'd had smoking carriages on trains, though not on the Tube. A ban subsequently came in that was extended to all Underground platforms – even those in distant stations connected by lines that ran above ground. And that was a good thing.

I had a long-winded journey home via St Pancras to Luton and then by cab to Stevenage – but of course I was lucky: many people would not be going home at all that night. If Heysel had not made me realise how fragile life can be, this was another stark reminder. And yet again I was left to marvel at the job our emergency services do in appalling circumstances.

One constant annoyance with commuting around that time was the constant interruptions to services caused by bomb scares. "Due to a suspect package..." was the frequent announcement. This was the time of the Troubles in Northern Ireland, which overflowed with horrific effects to the mainland all too often.

Six were killed in a bombing at Harrods in 1983; 11 soldiers were killed by a bomb in Hyde Park the year before. Then in 1985, there was the Brighton bomb, when the IRA tried but failed to kill Margaret Thatcher and her Cabinet, who were staying at the Grand Hotel on the seafront. Five were killed, including an MP, Sir Anthony Berry, and 31 were injured.

London's streets became trashcans when litter bins were removed, as they had been used by the bombers. These were jittery times and you were always on your guard against discarded items of luggage. I lost count of the times my Tube was halted, ending in a missed connection and late arrival home, which inevitably caused strife.

Little did we know it at the time but secret behind-the- scenes soundings to try to bring the Troubles to an end were underway despite constant proclamations from the Government about never negotiating with terrorists. They came about after a realisation on both sides that the British would not cave in, nor could they crush the terrorists, and the Republicans would not get their united Ireland. Both sides had to give.

I once toured Belfast to write a piece for an American publication. I drove up from Dublin, across the border and visited the scarred areas of the city. Tourist buses now go past the murals of William of Orange and iconised, balaclava-clad terrorists of both religious denominations and declarations of 'No Surrender'. But I noted there was an oppressive air to the place.

One lad in a pub near Windsor Park stadium explained that you never asked about religion. When you saw a girl you fancied, you could tell immediately by her name if she was Catholic or Protestant.

I never imagined that after 30 years we would have an open border between the harsh north and the beautiful south. And every effort should be made to keep it so.

I tried to avoid driving to London for work, though I had no alternative when it came to doing late shifts, mostly at the weekends. Besides the lack of trains late at night, the company on the last rattler was often unpleasant, to say the least. I would usually bury my nose in a book or newspaper and avoid eye contact. The London way.

I left the Sporting Life in 1989 after five years but continued to see a number of the lads when they did shifts at the Mail on Sunday, including Neil Cook. He edited the tabloid Sporting Life Weekender and was an excellent, well-connected journalist who started his career in Worthing. He had a meteoric rise. But he met a very mystifying end.

Neil had moved, via the Financial Times, and a brief spell on a new Maxwell racing paper in the States, where they went up against the Daily Racing Form, to be Editor-in-Chief of the Gulf Times, an English language paper based in Doha, Qatar.

I contacted him in early 2009, not long before I returned to the UK from a near five-year spell in New Zealand. There were few obvious work prospects back home, as the 2007-8 global financial crisis unwound but there was a sports job going at his paper in Doha. I didn't pursue it in the end as other work came up. That was the last I heard of Neil, until I read of his death in strange circumstances. I learned that he had died in either 2018 or 2019 – and nobody apparently knew if it was murder or suicide. His body was found in a river in Lisbon.

The story was that Neil had left Qatar in something of a hurry with a Ukrainian girlfriend, moved to Portugal and essentially went off the grid, hiding all his past ties – which included missing his daughter's wedding – and doing his best to lay low. It seems he had made some enemies in Qatar, a feudal state run by the al-Thani family.

Neil had only just been traced in Portugal by his son when the family got the dreaded knock at the door from police. It must have been utterly devastating.

To add to the mystery, there were no reports visible on the internet of a police investigation or even an inquest. The death of a British national abroad would have attracted news interest here, too. Yet it didn't. His old paper in Doha erased all the old photos of him glad-handing Qatari big-wigs, including the royals. You have to conclude that he pissed off some very important people and feared for his life.

He had always been good company and mixed in some pretty elite circles. He spoke little of his private life but did let slip not long after we met that he was dating an heiress to the Hershey chocolate business.

He married someone else, Sarah, and I recall meeting her only once, at a hunt ball in Buxton's Palace Hotel organised by our boss, Mike Gallemore. I hope she and her family have been able to get their lives back on track.

Neil had been a key figure in the Sporting Life's resurgence. The paper's future had been shaky even before my time there. In 1984, its circulation was low and there were constant battles with the print unions just to get a paper out on the streets each day.

Yet the newspaper also experienced a big surge in circulation in the late 1980s – the "Loadsamoney" days, lampooned by comedian Harry Enfield, when racing became trendy and a place for yuppies to flaunt their newly-acquired wealth.

It was not known what Robert Maxwell had in mind for the Life in 1984 after he took over Mirror Group. But it had an unparalleled store of specialist data that should have made the title valuable, including race records of horses, jockeys and trainers, and form information. It should have been made available on subscription – as with stock market data – and could have given the paper a stronger financial base and enhanced future prospects.

Maxwell took little obvious interest in the Life, even though it was read by some very influential types – the royals included – and he loved to bask in reflected glory. One day, he called George White, our managing editor, over to Maxwell House for a meeting. George was left waiting for several hours in his outer office – worrying about a pile of work he needed to get on with and calls to make – before being summoned by the great man over something that could have been done in moments on the phone. Mike Gallemore, a Mirror man through and through, George's successor, was another to get similar treatment from the Old Man, as they called him. Sometimes Maxwell would forget why he had summoned - or that he had summoned them at all.

George once got his ear bitten by Maxwell over a critical story we had carried about his attempts to merge the football club he owned, Oxford United, with Reading and create a new club, Thames Valley Royals. I got called on my day off to write a "correcting" supportive feature of some length because usual football writer was on holiday. It was a bizarre request but I got paid for my time. The merger never happened and Maxwell probably never even read my piece, such was his attention span. But it was the only time I had anything even indirectly to do with the man, thankfully.

Mike used to say Maxwell would be very hot on things for only a few minutes. You had to tough it out. But it must have taken a worrying time for him and others to work that out.

Roy Greenslade, who edited the Mirror in 1989, called Maxwell "impossible to work for – a mercurial man with a monstrous ego". And even Pandora Maxwell, estranged wife of Maxwell's son, Kevin, said there was "a fundamental dishonesty" about everything her father-in-law said and did.

The Sporting Life's demise was hastened by a costly libel dispute: the Top Cees affair, in 1995. It was alleged that jockey Kieren Fallon held the horse back in a race prior to it winning the Chester Cup at a higher starting price. Trainer Lynda Ramsden, her gambler husband Jack and champion jockey Fallon won £195,000 in libel damages – plus costs said to run to up to £500,000 from MGN. And, with the Racing Post's financial muscle and growing presence, as well as a general decline in sales and profitability, the Life was straining to stay afloat.

On Tuesday, May 12, 1998, after 139 years and 36,910 issues, the Sporting Life rolled off the presses for the last time and part of Britain's sporting heritage died with it.

Mirror Group merged the Life with the Racing Post, which was set up and run by the Maktoum ruling family from the UAE, but never delivered on its promise that the Sporting Life would return, other than in solely digital form, much diminished. Thankfully, some of the staff found work on the

Post – but many didn't. And, for them, the comfort of the Mirror pension they had been promised was not there. Truly cruel for a lot of very good people – 32,000 were in the scheme, which was so good that staff had labelled it the "mink-lined coffin".

Maxwell had pillaged the Mirror pension scheme to the tune of £400m, moving money between a web of his companies in order to shore up a failing business empire that was massively over-leveraged. His aim was to stave off demands from banks, notably Goldman Sachs, to repay loans worth millions. And, shamefully, there were no laws to prevent it. And still none today.

Thatcher' successor as Prime Minister, John Major, once held up Maxwell, a Labour MP for Buckingham in the 1960s, as "a beacon of British business" but his words came back to haunt him.

The least Major should have done in the aftermath of Maxwell's giant frauds was to ensure that pension funds could be ring-fenced, safe from predators. Barely half the money looted by Maxwell was made good by the Government, though the fund was restored by Mirror Group in the following years. It was too late for a number of ex-Lifers.

Much of Maxwell's empire was kept out of the public eye, run through a Liechtenstein entity – the Maxwell Foundation – and controlled by a Swiss lawyer, which is why the scale of the pension fraud emerged only after his death. Never was the nickname the "bouncing Czech" more apt (he was born Ján Ludvík Hoch in an area that is now part of the

Ukraine but was then in Czechoslovakia).

With the walls buckling on his empire in 1991 – he was publisher of the Daily Mirror, Sunday Mirror, The People, Daily Record, New York Daily News and a raft of other titles across the world, plus several book publishers, including Macmillan – Maxwell decided to take a break alone on his yacht, moored in Gibraltar.

It was the Lady Ghislaine (named after his daughter, who was recently arrested in the United States and faces charges related to disgraced financier Jeffrey Epstein's sex crimes).

Cap'n Bob had a real captain to do the actual sailing. They went via Madeira to the Canaries and he received several faxes en-route – all with bad and worse news about the state of his financial empire.

The evening after his arrival, November 5, 1991, he instructed his skipper to cast off for a cruise – and some time that night he went overboard. His body was recovered after a helicopter search.

There is lingering debate even today over whether it was suicide or murder. Mossad, the Israeli intelligence service, figures in at least one conspiracy theory. Former Mirror editor Roy Greenslade came out for suicide.

He told the Guardian: "Maxwell was a man who could not face the ignominy of jail, of being shown to be a liar and a thief. And he very much knew that was coming. So I am a suicide theorist. I believe he threw himself off that boat."

But Ken Lennox, the Mirror's senior photographer,

who identified the publisher's naked corpse after it was pulled from the sea, to spare Maxwell's widow Betty the ordeal, was convinced it was an accident. "I know it sounds crazy," said Lennox, "but he looked good. His hair was still slicked back, his complexion – he looked as if he was still alive." Apart from a grazed left shoulder, the body was unmarked.

"He used to get up at night and pee over the stern. Everybody knew this," said Lennox. "He weighed about 22 stone. The railings were just wire. So I think he lost his balance, he was very top-heavy."

An inquest recorded death by heart attack and accidental drowning – although three pathologists disagreed on the cause of death. Maxwell was buried, according to his wishes, on the Mount of Olives in Jerusalem.

His son, Kevin, inherited the title of Britain's biggest bankrupt, to the tune of more than £400m, following the pensions scandal. Kevin's then wife, Pandora, mother to their seven children, on hearing an early-morning knock and presuming it to be journalists, flung open a bedroom window and yelled: "Piss off or I'll call the police."

"We are the police," came the pithy reply.

Greenslade attended every day of Kevin and his brother Ian's eight-month trial for conspiracy to defraud and was pleased when they were acquitted. Both George White and Mike Gallemore said they got on well with Kevin and, compared with his father, he was a pleasure to deal with.

Whatever sealed Robert Maxwell's demise, it was nevertheless a cause of great celebration in High Holborn. I had moved to the Mail on Sunday by then – but the pubs around the Mirror had a bumper night to mark his passing. It was some party – some even came in on their day off. Quite the "tribute". The hand of fate had caught up with Maxwell. Before then, though, I was immersed in an adventure in which another hand took, well, a major part in fate of a sporting kind.

18 Messiah and Naughty Boy

Diego Maradona was both the Messiah and a very naughty boy. One moment of his villainy and 20 seconds of his genius was all it took to end the sporting adventure of my life – and etch a further page of infamy in England's chequered but mostly painful World Cup football history.

I say that's ALL it took – there was art and artifice, shock and awe, indignation and inspiration, all crammed into five astonishing minutes that shone an unforgiving and then adoring light on the enigma that will forever be Diego Armando Maradona.

England fans are still angry about the way the little Argentinian, who died in November 2020 from a heart attack, punched the ball past Peter Shilton in a 1986 World Cup quarter-final watched by thousands in the Estadio Azteca, and by billions more on TV – and got away with it.

Bobby Robson's players were still numb and indignant that their protests to the officials had fallen on deaf ears when Maradona struck again just a few minutes later with the "Goal of the Century". It is a moment immortalised in World Cup legend – and with a statue at Mexico City's Aztec Stadium.

It was June 22, 1986, in Mexico's capital, 7,300ft above sea level, on a day of scalding heat and not a breath of wind. I was one of 114,580 in the giant bowl for that high noon showdown, local time.

There were lots of heart-in-the-mouth moments – mostly involving Maradona, whether he was scything through the brittle England defence, being cut down, or wasting time by taking a breather by re-arranging the corner flag, as he did at one point. But there was late drama, too, as England finally turned up for nine minutes and almost got away with a draw to take it to extra-time. That would, in all truth, have been grand larceny.

How England had reached the quarter-finals will have had even the most one-eyed, tub-thumping fans scratching their heads. They had been beaten in their opening match and drew the next, in which they lost captain Brian Robson for the rest of the tournament to a shoulder injury and had another experienced midfielder, Ray Wilkins, sent off.

Bobby Robson's side thus seemed, after only two matches, destined for an early and far from pleasant return to home shores when heroics had, perhaps foolishly, been expected by so many. 'Twas ever thus – certainly since 1966, and perhaps even before then. Didn't we give the game of football to the world? Then surely the world was ours to rule?...

England, improbably, resurrected their spluttering campaign in their final group match, with a 3-0, Gary Lineker-inspired mauling of old rivals Poland that had the few thousand white-shirted fans in a soulless Monterrey arena dancing a joyous, giant conga on the terraces long before the end. The team had somehow limped through a group many had expected them to win at a canter.

England then had to see off a spirited Paraguay, which they did, 3-0 at the Azteca, in the first knockout stage, the round of 16. Then came the day Maradona brought their world crashing down.

The pocket genius brought about an Argentina victory as much through the sheer force of his incredible will and personality as anything. But he had this unmatched ability to play on the very edge yet not be at all troubled if he crossed that boundary. Added to a highly potent mix as we anticipated the game was the backdrop of a recent war between the two countries. Its overtones hung large over the encounter – as it has over subsequent ones between the countries. But let's backtrack a bit.

Nick Chapman spent many years working at The Sun, and we were colleagues on the sports results desk at the Mail on Sunday each weekend. He suggested going to Mexico – I hadn't given it a thought – but jumped at the idea. Nick, a West Ham fan, was a seasoned traveller with club and country. I was not. I had never followed England abroad and had been shaken by witnessing the tragedy at the Heysel the previous year.

On balance, though, I felt the cost and distance might put off some of the more seasoned travelling English idiots who forever seem intent on re-enacting long-past wars on foreign shores. I was wrong, but Nick and I had wisely decided not to stay with them and made alternative travel and accommodation plans, which worked out like a dream.

Mexico had not been meant to stage the World Cup in 1986 at all. It had done so in 1970 – a tournament many still believe the greatest and was won by the best international team in history, Brazil, and featuring their greatest player, Pele.

Colombia had secured the right to host the finals in 1986 but was an economic basket case, led by a president who rose to power aided by a terror group. FIFA, the game's governing body, brushed aside late substitute hosting claims from the USA, Brazil and Canada. Pele and Franz Beckenbauer had championed a US bid but Congress in Washington refused to back it.

There were vested commercial interests at play that saw a small group of FIFA delegates benefit hugely from TV and ticket revenues by taking the finals to Mexico. And you thought the Russian and

Qatar bids were dodgy for 2018 and 2022? General unrest and a volcanic quake and landslide that killed 20,000, led to officials in Bogota forfeiting the right to stage the greatest show on turf.

Europe, in the guise of Spain, had hosted in 1982, so it was South America's turn. In early 1983, FIFA decided that Mexico should take on the tournament. Yet it, too, almost had to step aside following a series of deadly, devastating earthquakes in late 1985.

This was the first World Cup to feature 24 teams. It had a 16-team knockout phase following six opening groups that sent home only eight participants. Three of the 24 were British – England and Northern Ireland, who came through the same qualifying section, were joined by Scotland, who got through after a play-off.

England, with a squad that included Gary Lineker, Terry Butcher, John Barnes, Peter Shilton, Glenn Hoddle and Bryan Robson, were based in Monterrey, a bleak industrial city in the north-east of the country, about 135 miles from the Texas border.

If the England fans were to run amok there, FIFA must have reckoned, it might almost go unnoticed – or even be treated as structural improvement. Bobby Robson's men were drawn in what was seen as an eminently winnable group, with Morocco, Poland and Portugal.

The Scots were led by Alex Ferguson. He took over after the heart attack that killed his boss, Jock Stein, in Cardiff in September 1985, just as the Scots had secured a vital qualifying group draw against Wales.

Their games were in Neza, a shanty town-cum-city (formally known as Ciudad Nezahualcóyotl), just outside Mexico City, and Queretero, in central Mexico. They had Graeme Souness, Gordon Strachan and Alex McLeish in their ranks and had qualified for their fourth successive finals – a far better record than England in that era.

I saw Scotland's final qualifying play-off match. It was in Australia, where I had been visiting family, and took my young Aussie cousins, Matthew and Darren, to the game at Melbourne's Olympic Park. The Scots had led 2-0 from the first leg in Glasgow in November 1985, with the winners over the two games going to the finals. Frank Arok, the Socceroos' coach, warned the Scots to pack their sunscreen for the return in December, saying the game would be played up country in extreme summer heat.

But instead it went to Melbourne, where you can get all four seasons' weather in the same day. While I was there we had 30+C temperatures – but also hailstones the size of golf balls that had my uncle Roger scrambling to cover his car bonnet with a mattress.

It was an evening kick-off, with a 30,000 crowd, and the Scots held out for a 0-0 draw, though Jim Leighton was the busier goalkeeper. It meant Scotland and their Tartan Army of fans would now be heading down Mexico way. That joy was short-lived, as the Scots drew mission impossible: a finals group with Denmark, reigning South American champions Uruguay and always-strong West Germany.

Nonetheless the Scots fans would be going in droves – some not to return, as had been the case after the 1974 World Cup in Argentina, after falling captive to local beauties who couldn't resist a big, ginger, half-burned man in a skirt.

The Northern Irish, managed by the scholarly Billy Bingham, didn't have it any easier, being pitched in with Algeria, Spain and tournament favourites Brazil. They were able to call upon stars such as Pat Jennings, Sammy McIlroy and Norman Whiteside.

But their most realistic chance of getting out of the group was seen as being one of the best third-placed teams. They were based in Guadalajara, in the west, playing their matches at the Jalisco Stadium.

With our decision to go to the big jamboree made, Nick and I scrutinised the draw for the opening groups and all the permutations that could follow. We then sorted an itinerary that meant we would stay in Mexico City and fly up and back to Monterrey for each of the three England group games. We reckoned England would get through their group and next play either in Monterrey again, possibly against the Germans, or in Mexico City if they were group runners-up, which is what we were betting on. It was a good shout, based on form and the fact Englishmen are always over-optimistic about their national team.

We stayed in the Hotel la Reforma, on a main

thoroughfare close to the centre of Mexico City, with supporters from several other nations. As the tournament progressed, each team's fans would be goaded with the refrain, "Adios Su Casa" – "Goodbye, You're Going Home" – as results went the wrong way. After England's first two games, we were convinced we'd be "Su Casa" soon enough, along with the Scots and Irish boys in a very British exodus.

Nick and I had both had permission from work to stay on for the three weeks we had booked – or longer if England were still in the tournament. My boss said, sarcastically: "Tell the cab driver to hang about at Gatwick for you and keep the meter running."

We arrived in Mexico City a couple of days before the tournament, to acclimatise to the heat and altitude, get over the jet-lag and find our bearings. We soon found the Zona Rosa, the "Pink Zone", known for its huge array of decent eateries, where we dined most evenings and met a great group of Scottish lads we were to hang around with. Only later did we find out that the Zona Rosa was the centre of the city's gay community. We tried to get the Jocks to go there one night with their kilts on, just to liven things up. But they were more streetwise than they looked.

The first couple of nights were mayhem... but in a loud, over-the-top carnival way. Not in a sort of El Día de los Muertos (Day of the Dead) fashion, though there were some pretty dead-drunk folk knocking about in the early hours. Each of those first evenings there was a massive, chaotic, street celebration in the central square, the Zocalo, aka Constitution Square – a place of gathering since Aztec times. It was a huge, pent-up release of emotion for the Mexicans after the devastation of the September 19, 1985, earthquake in greater Mexico City that killed more than 10,000 inhabitants.

The 8.0-magnitude quake caused enormous damage, running to billions of dollars, and up to 500 major buildings were destroyed, including 13 public hospitals – one with 2,300 beds. Some 900 patients were killed in the initial shock alone.

It was clear from our first hours in the city that this World Cup was to be a massively cathartic event that would help restore national pride - especially if the hosts could go deep into the tournament.

Mexico had a very good team, built around the brilliantly athletic striker Hugo Sanchez, of Real Madrid, who was the tournament's poster boy. There were giant billboards and life-size cardboard cut-outs of him everywhere.

The city was so vibrant that first evening. We could hear car horns blaring, and shouting and singing outside the hotel and went to investigate – and ended up getting a hand-up onto the back of a flat-bed lorry with some local lads as they headed towards the Zocalo. The revelry went on late into the night. There was no trouble, just two nights of intense partying.

We were almost glad the tournament started so

that we could get some rest, though I suspect there was an element of jet-lag in there, too.

By day, well the afternoon by the time we surfaced, Nick and I wandered about to see some of the city sights – Mariachi bands seemed to lurk in every small public square, and there were busy markets and an awful lot of white-painted breeze-block walls with the tournament logo – a chilli pepper called Pique – and national flags and greetings stencilled on them. There had not been time to rebuild after the quake, so walls had been put up to hide the rubble from their welcome visitors' eyes.

We visited the canals of Xochimilco, the last remnants of a vast water transport system built by the Aztecs. Colourful gondola-like boats took us on cruises while food vendors, artisans and Mariachi bands floated past on other vessels.

We also took a trip out to Teotihuacan ("the place where the Gods were created") – an abandoned city that was visited and revered by the Aztecs in the 1400s, though by then it was almost 1,500 years old. It once supported a population of more than 100,000 and, in 1987, was designated a UNESCO World Heritage site.

The place is dominated by the giant Pyramid of the Sun and the smaller Pyramid of the Moon, which we clambered and admired the ancients' engineering skills, without any modern-day tools. Other key structures include the Ciudadela (Citadel) and the Temple of Quetzalcoatl (the Feathered Serpent).

We and our new Pictish pals couldn't be accused of ignoring the not insignificant culture in the region while savouring an incredible football experience. And to think Nick and I would have missed it all had we stayed in the wasteland of Monterrey.

We were on a loosely-organised tour, with the offer from a rep each morning in the hotel of tickets for the next few days' games. I forget how much they were, but we didn't feel ripped off.

Jack Charlton was our star tour "host", though we saw the 1966 England World Cup winner and his wife, Pat, only a couple of times, once on the coach to see Northern Ireland v Brazil in Guadalajara.

We were ideally placed to follow all three home nations – and some of football's brightest talents. And determined to do so.

19 He Wears It Well

We gave the opening game, with its colourful pre-match ceremonials, a miss as that would have been a budget buster. As anticipated, it was a tame draw – as many of these curtain-raisers are – between Bulgaria and Italy, which we watched on TV in the hotel.

Our first game in the flesh was to see Argentina – and Maradona – beat South Korea 3-1 at the Azteca and we got back via the Metro in time to watch England's group opponents, Morocco and Poland, play out an uninspiring 0-0 draw, from which we took major encouragement.

Next day, June 3, we were off to Monterrey with a small knot of Portugal fans from our hotel for England's first match. It seemed they, too, had not wanted to stay in the same city as a lot of English nut-jobs; they had us instead.

They were in for a treat – the great Eusebio, a Portuguese national hero, was on our flight and he chatted and had his picture taken with them. Their day was complete when Portugal won 1-0 with a 75th-minute goal from moustachioed midfielder Carlos Manuel. England hadn't played that badly. They just squandered their chances.

Lineker was denied the best of the lot when he slid the ball past the keeper, Manuel Bento, only for a covering defender to pull off a last-ditch clearance. But, after going behind, England were actually lucky not concede again.

It was not the happiest of return flights for us – and a little painful at the hotel. The Portuguese fans were, to be fair, great company. They had their five minutes of fun at our expense and didn't gloat half as much as I imagine some England fans might have done if the result been reversed.

Our Scots pals were staying in a hotel just across from us. It was more the budget variety, as they prioritised spending their hard-earned cash on drink rather than a comfy bed for the night.

Jake was the kilt-wearing 6ft 2in member of the group. He and Nick were "kidnapped" one evening by some local kids driving a truck in the celebratory aftermath of Mexico's 2-1 opening win over

Belgium.

Nick recalled: "They drove us about 30 minutes out of the city and only brought us back after me and Jake drank an entire bottle of tequila (Jake managed at least 60% of it!)" Jake met a stunning-looking and decidedly upmarket Mexican lady and decided to stay with her after the tournament. As he said: "Look at the choice – it's the trawlers or the rigs – or this!" I think the lady in question came from a wealthy family and I am sure Jake's charm and a smile as wide as Loch Lomond would have won over her family, whatever their initial horror.

Nick described the rest of the Caledonian cast list: "There was Fergus Bain, who worked for Aberdeen Council and became a good friend. He and his girl-friend Louise came to my wedding a few years later.

"Next was Zico. I wish I could remember his real name, but he got his nickname because he met the great Brazilian player Zico at the airport when he ar-rived and persuaded him to swap t-shirts. He wore that shirt every day for about three weeks! Probably never washed it.

"Then there was Louie. He was the wiry, short-tempered one. A girl tipped a pint of beer over his head to start a brief scuffle with the Argentinian fans in the Hilton bar on the night of our quarter-final."

The lads had been in the same bar the night they met Rod Stewart – while I was back in our hotel room suffering with "Montezuma's Revenge". We later worked out it must have been from a washed salad – an easy deduction as all the Scots salad-dodgers had been fine.

And Raspy Rod? Well, it is a story that wears well. Nick said: "We first saw him in the Hilton when two German girls asked for his autograph. He said to them: 'Tell me who won the war and I'll give you an autograph'. They obliged – and so did he.

"The Scots lads got chatting with him and he asked if we'd like to go to a nightclub with him. The guys said 'yes' – but I declined. It felt like a Scottish thing and I didn't quite fit in! I stayed drinking at the Hilton. Rod left the hotel, got into a stretch limo and headed to the rear entrance of a nightclub in the Zona Rosa.

"The lads had left with him, jumped in the limo directly behind Rod's and joined him at the club. The agreement was, that if they acted as his body-guards for the night, he would buy all the booze.

"So," Nick was told by star-struck Jake next day, "they formed a ring around Rod whenever he danced, and pushed up either side of him whenever he sat down, to make sure no one could bother him.

"Unless, of course, there were some ladies he didn't mind bothering him.

"At the end of a long, boozy night, they got back in the stretch limos and returned to the Hilton. When Rod got out with a three young women and went in-side, the limo driver presented the boys with a bill for several hundred dollars. They did a runner!"

Next day, Nick and I went with our surprisingly fresh-looking pals to Neza to watch the Scots' game with Denmark. Seasoned drinking pros to a man... It was a strange half-hour cab ride.

The further we got from the city centre, the poorer the surroundings. Yet at every set of lights we stopped at, we'd be mobbed by groups of young children. It was doubtless because of the full "regalia" the Jocks were wearing. These kids thrust beaded bracelets through the windows at us, with no pleas for anything in return. They had the biggest smiles on their faces and yet were some of the poorest kids you'd see, many with torn clothes and bare feet.

They proffered autograph books to the lads, who jotted down some fictitious names – Rob Roy, Lassie, Denis Law, George Best, or even Clyde Best. They would not know that Clyde, the West Ham striker, was black.

We got to this far-from-salubrious stadium, with a capacity of only 18,000 or so, in the middle of nowhere and prayed the cab driver would still be there after the game. Amazingly, he was.

The return trip, with the 90-minute wait, cost us just something like US$10... we more than matched that with a $20 tip and couldn't not help but think how much that sort of service might cost back home, and felt pleased that we had made the guy's week.

The Danes won 1-0 with a goal by Preben Elkjaer Larsson in the second half. Even Nick's West Ham hero, Frank McAvennie, who came on as a sub with the Scots chasing a result, could not sniff an equaliser.

Our new pals were not too despondent – they were definitely beer glass half-full types. Nick and I needed to be similarly optimistic after our next trip – back to Monterrey for England's game against Morocco.

Peter Reid and some of the other England players came over to our section for a quick chat during the warm-up. They seemed relaxed and confident. Perhaps too much so. The Moroccans had spent 40 days in Mexico ahead of the tournament to acclimatise and played warm-up matches against local teams.

Their first-choice goalkeeper, Zaki, was picked to play despite struggling with "stomach cramps". I felt for him, I really did. If you rearrange the phrase 'the bottom falling out of your world', you'll get my drift.

England started badly, then fell away. Just before half-time, skipper Bryan Robson tumbled awkwardly, dislocating his already-damaged shoulder and had to go off. He was later seen watching the remainder of the action while wearing a sling. His World Cup was over.

It went from bad to worse when Ray Wilkins, already on a yellow card, disagreed with an offside call by the referee and threw the ball back in his direction. It was petulant. He was instantly shown a second yellow then a red. Playing with 11 men in humid conditions was a tough ask against the skilful Moroccans. Now England had to do it with only 10.

The game finished goalless. But that point, while hugely disappointing, would prove precious. It meant that, with other results going their way, they could still reach the knockout stage with a draw against Poland five days later when it had seemed they would have to win that one.

Nick and I were at the airport when we recognised the match officials in their blue-grey check tournament blazers. I bagged a picture of Nick going up to the ref, Gabriel González, showing him a red card (well, a sunglasses case). To his credit, the Paraguayan took it in good part. He must have feared the worst when he was approached at pace by a stubbly-chinned Nick in his England shirt! Match magazine used the picture when we got home.

Next day we went with the Scots to Queretero for their match against the Germans, this time by coach. The Sweaties were in their element when Gordon Strachan put them 1-0 up. It didn't last long – five minutes, in fact, before Rudi Voller equalised. Another just after half-time by Klaus Allofs meant it would be sorrows-drowning later.

Nick and I were in our usual haunt, the Hilton, when we were joined by the Danish squad after their 6-1 thrashing of Uruguay. It was a result that made the other fancied sides in the tournament sit up and take proper notice.

The reigning Copa American champions, who had beaten Brazil over two legs to win that crown, had been clinically swept aside by these great Danes in the heat of Neza stadium, which incongruously was overlooked from a distance by the still-snow-capped Mount Popacatepetl. You try saying that with a drink inside you...

The unheralded Danes, who booked their place in the knockout stage with this win, had the brilliant twin striking threat of Michael Laudrup and Preben Elkjaer, all twists and turns, and with electric speed. Laudrup scored one and made a couple, while Elkjaer helped himself to a hat-trick in a display of searing pace that won over the admiring locals.

Jesper Olsen also scored. He was no stranger to British fans since his move two years earlier to Manchester United, where he was joined by John Sivebaek. Jan Molby had a successful spell at Liverpool, while the Danes' captain, Morten Olsen (no relation to Jesper), by now 36, had been set to join him in English football – but for his dog.

I got chatting to Morten and mentioned that I was a Spurs fan, when he told me how he had been about to join Tottenham after they had beaten his Belgian club, Anderlecht, on penalties to win the UEFA Cup in 1984. "We had agreed the transfer terms and it would have been a great move for me as I am nearing the end of my career and would have liked living and playing in London.

"But I have an old dog and he would have had to go in quarantine for six months. It would have been cruel, so I said 'no' in the end, as Tottenham could not pull any strings with the authorities."

Instead, he joined FC Koln, in Germany, playing 80 games for them. It was Tottenham's loss. Olsen was a class act. He won 102 caps for Denmark and, between 2000 and 2015, managed the national team to another century of games; a very rare feat indeed. He might even have been a future Tottenham manager had he moved to north London and impressed.

The Danes had brothers Michael and Brian Laudrup, who had fun telling us they thought Brian Robson was the most over-rated player in Europe. Nick and I were at the World Cup as fans, with no Press accreditation, yet we were able to mix in a hotel with some of the tournament's stars. You could not imagine that being the case now. Teams are closeted in screened-off training camps, barely accessible to the media and their families, let alone fans.

We Anglo-Scots band of brothers hung out at the Hilton most days – they had a great rooftop pool – and I think we convinced the security staff we were actually staying there. The BBC used it as their base and we were in the pool one afternoon and saw former England midfielder Trevor Brooking, a pundit for the Beeb, on a lounger, reading a paper and soaking up the sun.

Nick was thrilled – West Ham royalty! I was only surprised he didn't go up and pester him. Sir Trevor, as he is now, will have had England v Poland in mind, as that was our next game.

There was history between the sides, notably the embarrassment of 1973, when the Poles held out for a 1-1 draw at Wembley that, with their earlier 2-0 win in Katowice, meant England failed to qualify for the 1974 World Cup in West Germany and brought down the curtain on Sir Alf Ramsey's tenure as manager.

A similar result this time and Bobby Robson would probably just about avoid getting his P45. But really, England needed to show some fire and quality to get themselves into the tournament.

More than that, they needed to play to a system the players were comfortable with and get Glenn Hoddle, their most creative midfield player, more involved. England had a very good defensive record but, looking back at some of the video, it was skin-of-the-teeth stuff and much was down to some fortunate blocks and last-minute toe-ends to keep their goal intact. They had looked vulnerable against both Portugal and Morocco, arguably the weaker sides in the group.

The Poles opened brightest, with Boniek a real pain. But suddenly England arrived. Kenny Sansom won the ball on his own goal-line and fed Hoddle. After a slick move, Lineker swept home from Gary Stevens' low, driven cross.

Then Peter Beardsley's curling pass was met on the half-volley by Lineker to claim his second. England were 2-0 up in just 15 minutes. Polish keeper Jozef Mlynarcyk helpfully dropped a corner right into Lineker's lap: 34 minutes gone and the game was done and dusted. All a bit different to 1973.

It meant England would finish second in their group and play Paraguay in Mexico City next. Nick and I had been soothsayers all along. England had achieved at least partly what they had set out to do – but world-beaters? No, they had merely potentially turned a corner. And we were just relieved our trip wasn't over prematurely.

Next day we headed to Guadalajara to see Brazil, who had beaten both Spain and Algeria. They had qualified for the next round and were up against Northern Ireland, whose tournament was realistically over.

The most memorable thing, aside from seeing the great Brazilians was the scoreboard before the game. The Brazil team was up there in lights – with all the players known by one name: Socrates, Careca, Junior, Branco, and so on. A small cultural misunderstanding saw the Northern Ireland team names lit up beside them as Pat, Jimmy, Mal, David, Norman, and so on. I have no idea if the Irish lads had noticed and were too busy laughing to keep out the brilliant Brazilians. Two crackers from Careca, a jolter from Josimar and it was a 3-0 stroll for Brazil, with Socrates – a thinking man's midfielder – a powerful guiding light. You had to see the Brazilians as strong contenders, especially as Poland, their knockout-round opponents, would not be interrupting their sleep.

With that, the group stages were over for us. After all this excitement we needed a holiday... so we went to a travel agent near our hotel and booked a two-night break in Acapulco. I can't see why Great Train robbers Buster Edwards and Bruce Reynolds would not have wanted to stay! Reynolds, the inspiration for the Michael Caine character Harry Palmer, was eventually nabbed in Torquay after five-years on the lam. He was played by Larry Lamb in the movie Buster, which starred Phil Collins as Edwards.

Turns out it was a cheap time of year to get away because the Americans tend to stay at home when it warms up in the States. So we went loco down in Acapulco… sun, sea, cliff-divers and all. Not in any pre-defined order. We lapped up the rays by the pool at a really smart hotel overlooking the Pacific before heading back to Mexico City for the business end of the tournament.

Acapulco used to be a hangout for Hollywood stars and a popular call-in for cruise ship passengers. But, since about 2014 there has been a spike in gang violence and kidnappings over drug turf, so tourism is now largely only domestic. It has one of the world's highest homicide rates. We only murdered a few beers.

Nick and I bagged tickets for Italy v France at the Olympic Stadium – the arena where, in 1968, American sprinter Tommie Smith did his single-gloved podium Black Power salute and his spring-heeled compatriot Bob Beamon almost cleared the long-jump pit in a single bound.

Italy, the defending champions, had by now been shorn of goalkeeper and team leader Dino Zoff, the ebullient Marco Tardelli, the brutal-tackling Claudio Gentile and goal machine Paolo Rossi – and, without that spine of steel, they were no match for the Gallic guile and panache of Michel Platini and Co, who cruised home 2-0 to book a quarter-final date with Brazil. Les Bleus should have beaten the Azzurri by more, in truth.

The following day it was England's turn to see if they could move up a gear. They were strong favourites to see off Paraguay, who had qualified behind Mexico in Group H. But a defensive brittleness was evident when an early Terry Butcher back-pass brought out some last-ditch heroics from Peter Shilton.

When Lineker, at full stretch, poked out a leg at the second time of asking to put England in front after half an hour, it seemed to uncork their fizz.

A brilliant save by Fernandez stopped a thumping point-black volley from Lineker after a slick Hoddle-inspired move.

Just after the interval, Lineker was cynically and brutally elbowed in the throat when he was off the ball and out of the officials' gaze. It was while he was getting medical attention off the field that Peter Beardsley struck from close range after the keeper spilled a shot from Butcher. Goal-hungry Lineker was doubtless thinking that would have been his strike had he still been on the field.

Twenty minutes from the end, Lineker rolled in a third to kill off the tie and make him the leading scorer at the World Cup, with five. Cue another England fans' conga. And cue Maradona...

20 Hand of God

There was history between England and Argentina even before the countries went to war over the Falkland Islands in 1982. In the 1966 World Cup quarter-final, a bruising, ill-tempered affair, Argentina captain Antonio Rattin was sent off but refused to go. He later claimed he didn't walk because he didn't understand what he was being told by the referee in English.

It shamed the tournament, the winners went on to lift the trophy – and red and yellow cards were introduced so there was no more Rattin on referees' decisions.

Sir Alf Ramsey, then just plain Alf, England's manager, branded the Argentina players "animals", refusing to let his players swap shirts at the end - and that rankled for many years in Buenos Aires.

The Azteca Stadium in 1986 was the first time that football teams from the two South Atlantic war opponents had met since the 10-week conflict four years earlier in which more than 1,000, mainly Argentinians, lost their lives. It was a war fought over a British dependency consisting of two main islands the area of Wales, inhabited mostly by penguins – plus 1,820 humans and 400,000 sheep.

Before the war, most Britons would have struggled to pick out where the Falklands were on a map, although Argentina has coveted the Malvinas, as they call them, since 1833 when a British naval force captured the territories from them. Post-war antipathy in 1982 ran so deep that it was not until 1989 that diplomatic relations were restored between the countries.

In Mexico City, tensions ran higher off the pitch than on it. On the Metro, fans mingled as they made their way to the stadium. I heard plenty of chanting but saw no nastiness or blows. Yet you sensed there was something intangibly menacing lurking just beneath the surface; a certain tenseness.

Inside the ground there was a potent cocktail of cold beer and pink Englishmen out in the midday sun. There were staff dispensing lagers in usherette fashion in the stands.

There were reports of a few fights outside the

ground, with England fans being hospitalised and their flags stolen, though I didn't see any trouble; and definitely not inside, despite areas where fans of both nations were intermingled.

Those purloined banners were apparently later shown off as "war trophies" by fans at Boca Juniors games – Maradona's former club.

But as the teams emerged into the brilliant sunlight, the Argentina players handed each England opponent their own personal pennant, in a small gesture of friendship; the high stakes, momentarily at least, were put to one side. This was sport, not war. A reality check.

In a tense first half, Argentina probed at will, with England showing little ambition to get on the front foot, and it made them appear somewhat leaden-legged, especially when Maradona ran at them from deep. He was skipping past challenges with alarming ease.

For the England defenders, facing the little man was like trying to nail jelly to a wall. His low centre of gravity and incredible balance and ability to change pace and direction in a split second made him the trickiest of opponents, even if you doubled up defenders on him.

It is a mystery how Terry Fenwick, for one, was not booked eight times at least as he tackled hard or late – often both, in an effort to subdue him. Maradona was Argentina's heartbeat and their energy source. Every threat stemmed from him. It was a masterclass.

There was little end product for Argentina, though, as England did enough to keep themselves in the game and tried to catch Argentina on the break.

Half-time came with the scores level and we were starting to think that, with a couple of judicious substitutions – "at least give John Barnes a go" we were urging – and cute tactical switches, we might be needing to extend our stay in the city after all.

We were also contemplating penalties after another deadlocked 45 minutes, enjoying another beer and working out who might take them. That illusion was shattered somewhat swiftly.

Even from my place in the stands at the opposite end of the stadium, it was clear and obvious that Maradona punched the ball into the England net after 51 minutes. I wasn't alone.

But I can, having seen the film numerous times, see how I had based my view as much on logic as the evidence of my own eyes. Even the TV commentators had been slow to call it correctly, thinking England were irate about an offside not being given and not handball.

Maradona side-stepped Hoddle and went on another probing run at the England back line, then passed to Jorge Valdano, who lost the ball. Steve Hodge tried to clear but succeeded only in scooping it skywards and backwards towards his own goal, the ball arcing high towards the penalty spot.

Maradona, who had continued his run, was in for the kill. He leapt towards Shilton's outstretched fist just as the keeper, a touch slow off his line, tried to punch the ball clear. Next thing, it was in the England net.

We were sure it would be chalked off. I suspect even Maradona thought so, too.

He later revealed how a couple of team-mates had asked him if he had handled the ball and he told them: "Shut up and keep celebrating!"

Every football fan knew that Shilton was 6ft tall while Argentina's captain was just 5ft 4in in stockinged feet. In physical terms, it was a mismatch. The England goalkeeper had his fist above his own head, but so too, did Maradona, though it went unnoticed by Ali Ben Nasser, the Tunisian referee.

Ben Nasser said later that he had waited for a signal from the Bulgarian linesman, Bogdan Dochev, who he believed would have had an unrestricted view of the incident, as he did. Since no signal came, Ben Nasser awarded the goal.

Dochev blamed Ben Nasser, saying that assistant referees were not allowed by FIFA to discuss any decisions with referees; that whatever the referee decided was final. Years later, Dochev said Maradona - that moment - had ruined his life. The controversy hung over him until he died in 2017. "Maradona is a brilliant footballer but a small man. He is low in height and as a person."

Shilton, Kenny Sansom, and Butcher protested loudly but Fenwick was the most vociferous, showing the referee what had happened, using a violent chopping-arm movement. The official was not persuaded. Methinks they did not protest too much.

Other England players were walking back for the restart, more accepting, but they likely did not have had such a clear view of Maradona's sleight of fist.

About a year later, I interviewed Gary Stevens when his Tottenham XI played a friendly against a Stevenage Sunday League XI.

He said of Maradona's goal: "I thought Shilts was odds-on to get it, next thing it was in the net. John Barnes, who was on the bench, said straight away it was handball. Some of the refereeing in Mexico was poor and that goal was a choker."

It was sly on the little Argentinian's part. Watching it back, it is not insignificant that the BBC's Barry Davies thought it might have been offside until he picked up on the protests by Hodge and Co.

Photos in the next day's newspapers showed that while Maradona had leapt powerfully, fully committed, Shilton was barely off the ground.

So there was some room for doubt in the officials' minds - and yet logic told you there was still no way Maradona could have headed the ball. Where's VAR when you need it?

It was a brutal blow. Maradona wheeled away in a chest-thumping celebration having got one over the old enemy. The fans below and round about us in sky blue and white were euphoric.

Surely, we couldn't go out of the tournament like this, though? A swift riposte was needed. But England were too angry and too shellshocked to repel

Maradona's next intervention.

Picking up possession in his own half, facing his own goal, he dragged the ball back, twisted away from Reid and then set off at pace, slaloming through the England defence. Fenwick, already booked, thought for a brief moment about bringing him down then backed off, Butcher, beaten once, then tried a last-ditch slide as Maradona sat Shilton down before pushing the ball into the net.

It took barely 12 seconds from the moment he collected the ball all of 60 yards out, and he beat his opponents in some instances with only a sway of his hips and without touching the ball.

It was poetry in fluid, entrancing extraordinary motion. The stuff of wildest dreams.

The goal looks ever more improbable with each replay. I didn't see the BBC coverage until later but Davies was a class act when he called it: "You have to say that is magnificent. There is no debate about that goal. That was pure football genius."

Gary Lineker, who witnessed the goal from the other end of the pitch, said later: "It's the only time as a player when I've felt like I ought to clap. I just thought, 'Wow'. If there was ever a man who dragged a team to win a World Cup, it was Maradona."

Asked about the first goal, Maradona said it was "a little bit Maradona, a little bit the Hand of God". Headline gold.

When we weigh up those goals, does one balance out the other?

No. History certainly remembers them both in

the same breath. For the English, it was a blatant injustice so hard to stomach that bookmakers William Hill paid out punters who backed the draw, in spite of the final score.

John Barnes' late introduction - surely too late - changed the complexion of the game and his clever run and beautifully-flighted, left-foot cross gave Lineker the chance to pull one back with nine minutes left. It was his sixth goal of the tournament, which won him the Golden Boot as top scorer.

It could so easily have been seven. As England went all-out for an equaliser, they left the back door open and Carlos Tapia's shot came back off the inside of Shilton's right-hand post and spun to safety. Still, Bobby Robson's men tried to push, push, urged on by Hoddle and Hodge plus the fresh legs and intuitive inspiration of Barnes.

For all their displeasure at Maradona's first goal, England should have been a man light for much of the encounter. Fenwick, booked for a loutish challenge on Maradona after just nine minutes, should have walked after tripping Valdano.

Then came another moment of Barnes magic down the left flank. He sold his marker and sent over a cross that somehow, agonisingly, eluded Lineker's lunging head at the far post. It could be that Julio Olarticoechea's close attention just did enough to put him off. The ball from Barnes skirted along the goal-line invitingly between the posts, after beating the less than convincing goalkeeper, Nery Pumpido.

Lineker didn't have long to reflect on a moment that might otherwise have given him nightmares. Nor was it to be a career-defining one, as he signed for Barcelona for £2.8m just after the tournament.

There was much ill-feeling among the players at the final whistle, though Hodge managed to swap shirts with Maradona (it was later donated to the National Football Museum in Manchester). Some wags said it was the closest Hodge had got to Maradona all day.

Butcher and the little man were drawn to provide post-match urine samples for routine drug tests. Butcher recalled: "He pointed to his hand. Probably the best thing he ever did, because I would have killed him if he hadn't admitted it."

Maradona has never apologised for that first goal. To understand that moment, you have to understand that in Argentina, it's often said that the only crime is getting caught.

People there like the first goal better than the second. "In the potrero (the poorer communities) the second goal is worth two," was Maradona's refrain. The informal rules of a street kickabout endure more than the formal rules of a World Cup.

Shilton cannot forgive or forget. He played in three World Cups and shares the record for clean sheets with Fabien Barthez, of France, after shutting out the opposition in 10 games. He also won the European Cup twice with Nottingham Forest.

"I did everything I could and the famous photo shows that I'm closer to the ball than his head.

That's why he punched it in with this hand

"You always have people saying: 'Oh, he out-jumped you.' He didn't out-jump me. He cheated. The whole England team suffered because he cheated. He admitted to it in a roundabout way. But he didn't ever show any remorse."

Shilton turned down a request from Maradona a few years ago to appear alongside him on a TV programme. "We've been offered a number of times to put it to bed. But he won't apologise so I won't shake hands with him or acknowledge him.

"I always say he's the greatest player in history – but I don't respect him as a sportsman and I never will."

And the second goal? "It was typical of what he could do," Shilton admits.

"But we weren't in the right frame of mind after what happened. Before the ball broke to Maradona, Glenn Hoddle was fouled so we should have had a free-kick. But you can't take anything away from him."

In any case, for Shilton and his team-mates, for Nick and I, it was 'Adios Su Casa".

But what memories...

21 All Systems Go

I had been working at the Life for five years and also been doing shifts at the Mail on Sunday, alongside Neil Cook, Dave Dibben – a brilliant operator from Mirror sport – as well has Steve Clemens, another Mirror sub, who would come on our MoS golf jollies to Norfolk.

One day we were on a break in the Harrow pub across the road and Phil Jordan, a senior reporter, and John Forbes, a news sub, asked me if I would be interested in joining them in a new department being set up at the MoS: Editorial Systems. The remit was to assemble a team of journalists to train and support staff on the new publishing systems that would replace the printers.

It wasn't a hard sell. I have always thought it important to take any training that is going, in order to stay current and even to get ahead of the tech curve. I'd advise anyone else to do the same. It can help make you more employable for longer.

They heard I was interested in tech at a time Mirror Group was beginning to bring in desktop publishing, and they wanted someone with a sports background. I considered the idea for about three nanoseconds. In fact I halted the sales pitch when they said I would have to go to California for six weeks, with Club Class flights, be put up in a Hilton for the duration and do a series of courses on a system that we would soon be replacing. What was not to like?

Phil said it would give me a good grounding in what to demand from a system from an editorial point of view – and enable me to be aware of how we might transition from one system to the new one for the benefit of the staff, not the kit salesmen.

It was a wonderful trip. I didn't need to do one of the courses, on programming, so I had a spare week, which I took as holiday and boarded the Amtrak train to see my brother Kevin and his wife Bridget in Indiana. It was so much better than a flight, though I caught a plane back to save time. I got to see backyard America, with its small towns and varied landscape – the mountains and rivers, the plains and towns with those distinctive water towers bearing the place name.

I got a real sense of scale and geography; it was the best school field trip ever. And I was surprised by how many more "soccer" fields I saw along the way than American football grids. It hinted at how the game was catching on there.

The views were stunning from the California Zephyr, which I boarded in Sacramento, where I was staying. It wound through the Rockies, the Sierra Nevadas, through Reno, Salt Lake City, Denver and Omaha to Chicago, crossing both the Mississippi and the Missouri rivers along the way (which was news to some of the Americans I spoke to on board, who had no idea of their own country's geography). It is astonishing how few Americans travel out of their state, let alone have a passport and go abroad. That is perhaps a clue to how the Trump slogan, "Make America Great Again" got so much traction. So many Americans are insular; their yard is their entire world.

The courses offered a way of meeting people from newspapers in the US and Canada and I socialised with some from Los Angeles and Buffalo, playing golf one weekend with a bunch of them and touring the Napa Valley wineries and San Francisco on other occasions. Another time I went to Los Angeles, taking in Venice Beach, where there were roller-bladers and chainsaw jugglers and lots of toy dogs too tiny to walk so they were carried along in all sorts of contraptions, including some towed behind bikes.

John Forbes was just finishing his series of courses

when I arrived for mine and we met in San Francisco for the most unique Systems Department lunch you could imagine, at an Italian restaurant in Girardelli Square. It was a strange time to be in the city, though, a few weeks after the big earthquake, the Loma Prieta, that struck the Bay Area of California on October 17, 1989. It killed 63, with nearly 3,800 injured, and the damage it caused ran to US $6 billion. It also spawned some amazing stories of people being rescued from the rubble, including one guy who got so dreadfully pissed and, fearing the wrath of his wife, apparently climbed *into* the debris, where he was found, so he had a heroic story to tell her when he was 'rescued'.

After lunch with John, I drove north to Sacramento and could not take the direct route via the Bay Bridge, which had pancaked, and instead went over the Golden Gate to pick up the interstate north. Poetically, just as I drove over it, Simon and Garfunkel's Bridge Over Troubled Water came on the radio. Sadly, they didn't follow up with some Johnny Cash as I went past San Quentin prison.

There were a series of courses at System Integrators (SII) in Sacramento, the Californian state capital. In many ways it was a Rolls-Royce of a system for editors and writers. But the output of pages and stories still required the presence of compositors in the print room.

We were going over to using Macintoshes running PageSpeed – a new program devised in Provo, Utah – which demanded a two-week trip out there later.

I learned the system, then had to devise a training schedule for our staff and do the courses at our offices in Kensington or, for bigger groups such as the Saturday sports casuals, at our back-up offices in London's Surrey Quays, above the print plant.

Provo is Mormon country and home to the Osmonds' recording studios and Brigham Young University. BYU – or just the Y, as it is also known – is owned by The Church of Jesus Christ of Latter-day Saints (LDS). Utah is a dry state and I felt very grubby collecting a bottle of beer from the hotel shop in a brown paper bag, to drink in my room one Sunday.

My hosts at DTI were a cheap date when you took them for a meal. They only drank water. To be respectful, I did likewise. One evening, I went to eat at the Tree Room at Robert Redford's Sundance resort nearby, a venue for a big annual film festival. There really is a tree in it!

I suffered a major embarrassment in Sacramento, on the first of my US business visits. On Monday nights at the Hilton, they had a big screen in the lounge showing the big NFL football game of the weekend. Every time a touchdown was scored, out came the free shots. It was, fatefully, a high-scoring game.

I discovered I quite liked Long Island Iced Tea (vodka, tequila, light rum, triple sec, gin and a splash of Coke for colour). What I didn't like was feeling like death warmed up the next day. It was the worst I have ever been with drink. I am amazed

I found the lift let along my room key. Worse, I had been sick all over my bed. That was an awkward conversation at reception. I did at least tip the maid handsomely.

I was left red-faced, too, on a later trip to Provo. With not much to do one weekend, I hooked up with some Canadian dentists who were staying in the hotel – where Tom Cruise and his then-wife Mimi checked-in one Sunday. Wow, someone even smaller than me...

The guys persuaded me to go skiing. They might just as well have suggested being Tom's Mission Impossible stunt double. You know, for stepping off a kerb or something. I had never been before, but they said they would look out for me and I could book a lesson while I was there. We went to Park City, which is where the US Winter Olympic teams train. A gentle initiation, then... with my rented skis strapped on firmly but feeling like awkward planks under my feet. I'd had to buy gloves and a warm jacket (amazing what you could drop in on expenses back then!), as I was ill-equipped in every sense.

I rode the cable car with the chaps to the top of the mountain, just for the view. They got off and I carried on back to the ground, where I had a lesson booked. As I waited, I thought I would give it a go myself, trying to ski down first from five yards up the slope, then going a little higher. I got to about 20 yards and was feeling ready for a black run to the sound of cowbells. But, in my cockiness, I lost control – just as a very expensively kitted-out family were about to cross my path.

The glass-fronted park cafeteria was right behind them. I managed, I have no idea how, to 'snow-plough' and stop, falling on my behind – but it was close. The group scattered just as I had visions of an X-shaped hole appearing in the plate glass. So I 'retired' until my lesson. I'd had all the adrenaline I could take. I had the lesson, was no better – and that's why I never halt long at the ski holiday brochures in the travel shop.

My poor training "victims" back at the office in London were brilliant. I'd never taught anything before, not since work experience in my old infants' school, and I am sure to the first few I must have come across as being a bit disorganised. It was the swan thing, really –

But I knew my stuff and was able to explain things on their level, which I think was appreciated – unlike many an outside trainer I have known. The hardest bit was training pairs where one person needed more help and support than the other. I learned on the hoof, keeping the quicker ones busy with tasks so they could use their initiative and thus buy time to help the stragglers.

Not everyone takes to tech easily. I have seen people pick the mouse up, failing to grasp that the cursor didn't move until they put it flat again. Or open the CD tray, thinking it was a cool coffee cup-holder. It is hard but essential to not use too much jargon. It throws people.

After that it was a matter of providing support on

press day, with sport my main domain. There would be a variety of problems, from user error to genuine software glitches – inevitably just as the pages were about to go to press. We always seemed to find a workaround or unorthodox fix: the pages never went out blank.

There was one occasion when news were about to send a financial spread about bankers Morgan Grenfell. The sub, as taught, did a last-minute spellcheck – but hit the wrong button and replaced the words "Morgan Grenfell" with "Organ Greenfly", the closest dictionary-suggested alternative. Luckily it was spotted and fixed.

One of the oddest incidents was when I was handed the task of setting up a disaster contingency suite at Surrey Quays. I occasionally had to go down there to check it was all good. Then one day, Executive Editor George Woodhouse suggested we have a dummy exercise there.

So about a dozen of us travelled in a minibus to the Docklands and were just setting up when we heard there had been a bomb threat back at base and our offices had been sealed. We were put on alert to produce pages for the Evening Standard if they could not get staff through the doors. We were stood down not long after, thankfully, so we knocked out a few dummy pages and headed back to Kensington having proved the site and the kit was fit for the task.

Phil Jordan left to go to the States, and Frobes, as we called John, took his place and I became his deputy. As our department grew, so did the demands for more tech across the newsroom – including reporters and photographers in the field on laptops.

This was before what we would now recognise as notebook computers. The best on offer was a basic Tandy machine that had a word processor and could be programmed to transmit stuff to the office. And there was no internet at this point. You had in stick a cable into a phone jack.

The ability for photographers to take and transmit their photos was a huge advance, though initially they had to develop their film first on site and scan the film into a laptop. The digital cameras of the time were not good enough to deal with speed and poor light like film. They were way inferior to the average smartphone today. Sometimes we had to support the snappers on site, such as in Portsmouth for a D-Day anniversary event.

Being able to send pictures from an event changed coverage. Before, we would get a photo from the first half of a football match and the film was biked back to the office to be developed. Now they can send it back via Wi-Fi or a data connection.

There were many changes to the production process: some subtle and some major, such as the digital pairing of pages for print; colour enhancement using Photoshop; and it was easier to do typographical tricks that could bring pages alive, adding shadows, cutting out parts of an image or whole shapes. But our pleadings to management regarding the fledgling internet went unheeded for years and foreshadowed to some extent the conundrum papers have found themselves in today.

In our small department, we had modems on our desk, then ISDN lines (digital lines as opposed to slower modems) and, with the first broadband connections on the horizon, we could foresee how this might radically change publishing. We used to imagine, on our boozy lunches, all manner of Tomorrow's World things.

Gurmail Dhaliwal, our programming expert, dreamed up a virtual shopping mall where your avatar would wander around and you could meet and chat with others – or duck into a shop, view their catalogue and order online. Online ordering barely existed back then – though you could buy books from a small company you might have heard of, Amazon. He was a prophet. But we were never able to turn it into profit...

Phil had this notion that with pages across Fleet Street all digital, people on cruise ships could order personalised news sheets from their cabin – the Guardian front page, page three of the Sun and the Telegraph crossword. Ships now do stuff like that, though without the naughty bits.

They were fertile times. An exciting world was opening up, it seemed. I used to have a Tomorrow's World book when I was a teenager but sadly no longer have it. It would be interesting to see how many of the things they predicted in the 1970s came true, you know, like mobile phones.

Phil, John and I were internet evangelists, saying

this was something the papers needed to be all over like a cheap suit. The time was right to make all the mistakes while nobody was looking, and to mark out our territory in cyberspace. Nobody in authority would take it on. I suspect they just didn't comprehend it. But that wasn't only true of our management – too many others missed the boat, and the industry was failed by them.

I worked for the MoS for more than 30 years, on and off – as a casual, full-time and part-time. Returning always felt like coming home, particularly after a five-year stint in New Zealand. The building in Kensington has an impressive atrium with glass lifts and the whole thing looks impressive as you go up the escalator to the main reception. It always felt a privilege to work there.

What struck me on my return was how I must have treated people decently. Two of the security guards greeted me on my first shift for five years, remarking that they hadn't seen me for a time, what had I been doing? Then one of the canteen ladies welcomed me back with a broad smile and a similar query. That meant a great deal. Everyone in a company should be treated with respect – and, having seen some self-important types in Northcliffe House down the years, it was clear from the lady's greeting that she hadn't always had universal appreciation.

I'll admit that I have never been the best sub, best writer or best in the tech field – but I do have a breadth of competence that has enabled me to endure in a turbulent industry. My people skills, which I showed on my first paper, in Hitchin, have always stood me in decent stead.

Doing or saying the right thing didn't always have its rewards, mind you. I was once banned from Stevenage Athletic for reporting how the Player of the Year award was re-allocated when the intended recipient couldn't go to the ceremony. My sources were trusted but the chairman chewed the editor's ear and I got it next. It was all smoothed over before the start of the next season and I never had to provide a match report by looking through the stadium fence. It was a pity, in some respects. Banning the media never looks good and is counter-productive. I also got bawled out at Letchworth FC after I reported how a car with four of their best players broke down on the North Circular on the way to a game when that could have been avoided by using a team coach. The chairman, Sid Smith, fronted me in the bar after a match one evening with my chief reporter Barrie Dack there. Sid was upset that the club would now have to run to the cost of hiring coaches.

He rounded on Barrie, saying he'd "sent a boy to do a man's job". But I stood my ground and asked if anything I had reported was untrue. There was silence. It wasn't wrong, I knew – because I had been in the car with the players. The game would have had to be abandoned if the players didn't eventually get the car going, even if they arrived a bit late, in Erith, I think it was. Barrie talked Sid round and I even ended up going on the team coach to future matches, particularly FA Cup ties.

Some young reporters blunder in and get the door slammed in their face. Today, trainees are taught the importance of even minor details such as dress... how actually *not* wearing a jacket and tie might be more appropriate in some circumstances.

The foot-in-the-door merchants are a wonder to behold, and I am sure we're all familiar with photographers mobbing someone for that one special snap – or being intrusive with a long lens.

The royals were often ripe for that. And the press, in particular paparazzi snappers, were certainly at the centre of the story the night Princess Diana died.

22 People's Princess

I t was the week Britain collapsed into a collective emotional mush – and, at one point, was
sorely tempted by the idea of seeing an end to
a monarchy that, under the unrelenting glare of an
unforgiving media, was exposed as being hopelessly
anachronistic and lacking in empathy and sincerity.

The country was tipped towards the edge, not by
political injustice or abuse of power, as it had in
the past, but by the sudden and shocking death of
a princess: the former wife of one future king and
mother to another. It was August 31, 1997 – a date
forever chiselled into the consciousness of millions

around the globe.

Diana, erstwhile Princess of Wales, was the tabloids' Queen of Hearts. Or the "People's Princess" – a label coined by the new Prime Minister, Tony Blair (more accurately, by his spin doctor Alastair Campbell).

Many ordinary people felt that she spoke directly to them, as a doting mother, a scorned wife and champion of many worthy causes – from the removal of landmines to the fight against Aids, homelessness and poverty.

She had qualities that Britons had hoped to see in their future king's consort. They had also hoped her finer qualities would seep under the skins of the royals, without them having to be verbally waterboarded by public opinion and the media to get with the times. It was a vain hope.

Did Charles ever look more ill at ease than when he went with Diana to Live Aid in July 1985, which I attended with half a dozen people from the flats in Stevenage where I was living? She was in a light blue summer dress and Charles was out of place in a double-breasted suit and tie. She had Phil Collins and Brian May for company while he had the Geldofs in his ear, Bob doubtless saying how the Dubai rulers had chipped in and would he, too, mind "giving me the fucking money".

The princess was a troubled soul, deeply scarred by a marriage that seemed doomed from the off. When she died in a car crash in central Paris early that Sunday morning, it unleashed a torrent of public grief, regret and anger that the country had not witnessed for years, perhaps not in living memory.

It was a national drama as large as her life, played out before a global audience. And in many ways, it redefined the people's relationship with the Royal Family.

Diana had been a fixture on our front pages and on the covers of countless glossy magazines ever since word got out that a shy, 19-year-old blue-blood might finally be "the one" for the heir to the British throne – selected for him or otherwise.

The heir's oats had been sown and now was the time to secure the line of succession with an heir and a spare. It was a whirlwind courtship that included, if the tabloids were to be believed, some quality "alone time" on the royal train as it was parked up in the sidings. Tunnels and trains, eh?

The mass media began to follow every twist of Diana's life – the teenager in the see-through dress, the casual hair-flicking and coy blushes – then the fairytale wedding at the Abbey with a dress that sported a train almost as long as an InterCity 125; motherhood to two boys and, devastatingly, her husband's thinly-disguised infidelity.

There followed the kiss-and-tell primetime TV revelations about "a marriage of three people", a barbed reference to Camilla Parker Bowles, Charles' long-time mistress; a confessional book by Daily Mail reporter Andrew Morton – Diana: Her True Story; the princess's battles with bulimia; a torrent of paparazzi pictures of her supposedly private moments, and staged photo-ops, such as the one of Diana seated alone outside the Taj Mahal – a building of wonder, constructed as a tribute to eternal love.

On a hot August night, it all came to an end in a few violent seconds, followed by one of the most turbulent weeks in Britain's social history – and one on which the conspiracy theorists could seriously set to work. It was claimed that Prince Philip had ordered "a hit" because the mother of the future king was dating a "forriner" – and that she was pregnant with Dodi Fayed's child. Some reports suggested Dodi was about to propose to her and had bought rings in Paris.

The bottom line in the conspiracy world was a presumed shame having been brought upon the House of Windsor by a young woman who had never properly fitted in and had to be done away with as things would only get worse.

Kings-in-waiting had traditionally had a wife for respectability while getting their kicks elsewhere, though in Charles' case, it seems he had always been besotted with Camilla and marriage to Diana was not going to interfere with that relationship. Choosing Diana, it seemed, had been a royal tick-box exercise. The new baby machine had been vetted, bedded – then left to her own devices.

Charles and Camilla had been out of sync. She was married while he was single, that marriage in itself making her unsuitable to be his consort. But even when both were in wedded relationships, neither of those was respected and they went their merry way, continuing to see each other and construct their own private world unaffected by reality.

The conspiracy theorists who came out of the woodwork after Diana's death were resolutely cloth-eared to the findings of numerous investigations, with a host of experts agreeing the official line: that Diana died in a car driven by a man who was drunk (and who was not even a chauffeur but head of hotel security). To the disbelievers, there had to be a more otherworldly reason why such a widely-adored woman's life was cut short so cruelly.

The report into Diana's death examined 175 theories about what happened that night. It found none was true. And yet many claims rage on, even to this day. Some of the more anti-establishment ones were propagated by Dodi's father, Mohamed Fayed, the Egyptian owner of Harrods.

I was working the 'graveyard shift' (perhaps a poor choice of term in this instance) at the Mail on Sunday, providing technical editorial back-up. I started at 5pm that Saturday and was due to finish at 3am, just after the last opportunity we normally had to print a few late copies for limited city-centre markets (plus the editor's letterbox). But it wasn't until the Sunday afternoon that I finally left the office as an extraordinary story unfolded. And it continued even as I drove back to my home, at this point in Northamptonshire, not too far from Diana's family pile and where she would be buried.

It had been a pretty routine day on sport, where I was stationed for the early part of my shift. The Premier League was in full swing: champions Manchester United beat Coventry 3-0 at Old Trafford, the North London derby between Spurs and Arsenal was goal-less and Derby County beat Barnsley 1-0 (yes, both teams were in the top division). Greg Rusedski, the Canadian Brit, was hammering down 140km/h (86mph) serves at the US Open tennis in New York and the cricket season was winding down after a home Ashes defeat for England, and Glamorgan about to win the County Championship for the first time since 1969.

Will Smith's Men in Black was top of the charts, heading off Tubthumping, by Chumbawumba, and it had been a decent year for movie fans, with Titanic, Air Force One, The Full Monty and As Good As it Gets hitting the nation's big screens, as well as the new Bond: Tomorrow Never Dies – Pierce Brosnan's second outing as 007.

By 11.30pm, the MoS newsroom was quiet, with just a few duty reporters, sub-editors, picture desk and art desk staff. The execs had gone home, as had sports desk.

At 12.23am UK time, a black Mercedes driven by Henri Paul, with Diana, her boyfriend Dodi Fayed and bodyguard Trevor Rees-Jones aboard, slammed into a concrete pillar in the Pont d'Alma tunnel beneath the Seine in central Paris, then spun and ricocheted into a facing wall in a crash that left two of the occupants dead, one critically hurt and one seriously injured.

They had been pursued at high speed by paparazzi on scooters and motorbikes after leaving the Ritz Hotel, which was owned by Dodi Fayed's father, and headed for a family property in the Paris suburbs. Computer-aided impact reconstructions suggested they hit the 13th pillar in the tunnel at up to 120mph, experts said.

Later, freelance photographers who had been at the crash scene were arrested (they were in the clear once blood tests revealed Henri Paul had been drunk), while their bosses were vilified and subjected to death threats. The photos taken that night and hawked around newspapers by the agency Big Pictures would never be published.

The last photo from before crash was carried by The Sun. It showed Paul driving, Rees-Jones peering at the cameraman in front from below the passenger-side sun visor. Diana was side on – as if watching out for paparazzi behind. But no evidence was found that the snappers were near the car when it crashed.

Prince Harry, speaking many years later, described his torment. "William and I know that, we've been told she'd had a... quite a severe head injury, but was still very much alive on the back seat, and those people that... that caused the accident, instead of helping, were taking photographs of her dying on the back seat. And then those photographs made their way back to news desks in this country."

In the immediate aftermath, with the Press

being targeted for blame, the Mail editor-in-chief Sir David English announced the group would no longer purchase pictures taken by paparazzi. Yet if you look at MailOnline now, the whole operation is fuelled by pap shots.

It was only when news that driver Henri Paul was proven to be drunk that the blame began to shift yet the papers tore up forests for the newsprint they would use over the next week. The Evening Standard, for example, did a 44-page special that Monday and every paper did pull-outs, wrap-arounds and ate up acres of space with their Diana coverage.

They reprised all the famous old photos and her triumphs and tribulations. They were more coy about how the media clamour may have contributed in some way to the tragedy.

I briefly saw some of those pap shots when the MoS received them on our digital picture desk, touted by the agency, Big Pictures. I know from colleagues that picture desk staff elsewhere could not bring themselves to look at them, while some shed tears.

The handful I saw were enough for me to conclude that Diana had been fatally injured because she had not been wearing a seatbelt and suffered "percussion" injuries as a result. One crash expert likened the impact for passengers as "being thrown around like a missile".

But let's retrace her steps and look at how this massive global story unfolded:

Diana and Dodi had become close only six weeks before their deaths. They were pictured aboard his superyacht, Cujo, in the Med during the week, before heading to Paris. There were long-lens shots of Diana excitedly greeting her sons on board, and of her in a light blue, one-piece swimsuit, seated alone and looking almost mournful at the end of a diving board on the boat.

A "bounty" of up to £500,000 was being offered for anyone who got a photo of the couple kissing.

Dodi began dating Diana in July and had been holidaying with his American fiancée Kelly Fisher, a Calvin Klein model. He was said to have been sleeping with Kelly on one of the Fayed boats, Jonikal, while courting Diana on the other.

On July 29, Diana was with Dodi and toasted the first anniversary of her divorce from Charles, after four years of separation, in which she had to surrender her official status of Her Royal Highness, despite being mother to a future king.

At 3.35pm on Saturday, August 30, time-stamped CCTV showed Diana and Dodi arriving at the Ritz, entering through the back door. They made their way to the Imperial Suite, Room 102. Just before 6pm, the couple slipped out the same rear entrance in Rue Cambon and headed to his apartment near the Arc de Triomphe. Henri Paul drove them and went off duty. He was called back to the Ritz at 9.08pm. Just before 9pm, the couple were back at the Ritz, entering through the front doors. They headed for the hotel's l'Espadon restaurant. Diana reportedly ordered Dover sole, vegetable tempura and a mushroom and asparagus omelette. Dodi was apparently suspicious that photographers might be posing as patrons and asked for their food be delivered to their suite.

At 9.20pm, Dodi spoke to Paul and two Ritz chauffeurs. Paul was seen chatting to photographers shortly afterwards. At 9.43pm, Paul entered the Ritz's Bar Vendome, leaving with bodyguard Trevor Rees-Jones some 25 minutes later.

It was by now 11.51pm and a Mercedes and Range Rover were sent on a dummy run to try to draw away waiting photographers. Some 15 minutes later, just after midnight Paris time, Diana and Dodi left the Imperial Suite, intending to travel to back to the Arc apartment.

They could be seen on CCTV, smiling and joking. In the lobby, Dodi placed his arm around Diana's waist. She was wearing a long black jacket and white chinos, Dodi what looked like a tan suede jacket with tassels and fashionably ripped blue jeans.

At 12.20am they finally got into the Mercedes and were driven away, followed by at least three photographers on motorbikes. Paul was behind the wheel of the black Mercedes S280. He hadn't expected to be needed again after the couple went upstairs for dinner, and had been drinking and had at least two Ricards (an aniseed drink).

Paul was a 41-year-old bachelor who was being treated privately for alcoholism but was regarded as a loyal employee by the Ritz, where he was acting head of security and had ambitions for the appointment to be made permanent.

The inquest jury heard evidence that he had driven recklessly earlier in the day when he ferried some members of the Fayed entourage into Paris from the airport. But he was not qualified to be a chauffeur and was not used to driving the big Mercedes – his own car was a Mini.

Then there were issues with the car itself. The car's first owner, advertising tycoon Eric Bousquet, bought it in 1994. It was stolen three months later, and found in a field near Paris's Charles de Gaulle airport with signs that it had rolled several times. The vehicle was then overhauled and in 1996 went on sale at a Mercedes dealership in Paris.

Etoile Limousine bought it for around 40,000 euros and leased the car to the Ritz Hotel for use by its VIP guests. But the high-end limousine company realised very soon that there was a problem, that the car handled very badly at speeds higher than 70 to 80 kilometres per hour (43-50 mph). The firm sent the car back to Mercedes to resolve the problem.

The vehicle was stolen a second time four months before the accident and then abandoned on a motorway. It underwent 17,000 euros worth of repairs before rejoining the Etoile Limousine fleet and the Ritz garage where it was selected to chauffeur Diana.

Dodi had apparently told Rees-Jones to go in a decoy vehicle. He objected strongly and it was only at the last minute that Dodi relented. Paul was eventually found to be more than three times over

France's legal limit, and analysis of blood, hair and spinal cord later detected the anti-depressant Prozac as well Tiapridal, often used to combat alcohol withdrawal.

At 12.25am, the speeding car collided at more than 80mph (some reports said 125mph) with one of a series of concrete pillars in the Pont de l'Alma tunnel, which had a 30mph limit. The impact was concentrated on the left front (driver's side) but the car whipped violently anti-clockwise, to come to rest against the inside lane's concrete wall and halt almost facing the way from which it had come.

It may have just clipped a white Fiat Uno, which then had to swerve to get past the wreckage but did not stop. Despite a nationwide hunt, the Fiat was never found.

Seconds earlier, Rees-Jones had buckled his seat belt, which went against typical procedure for bodyguards as they need to me mobile quickly in the face of a threat. He would be the only one to survive.

Paul and Dodi, who had been on the side of the car that took the impact, were dead at the scene. The trailing photographers were soon at the crash site, with more arriving later as news of the tragedy spread.

One of the first snappers opened the rear door Diana's side, while the next stopped to take a few shots before they headed off with their film. In the images I saw, Diana was sitting in the footwell in front of her seat, with her back to the door and head against Rees-Jones' seat.

By chance, a doctor, Frédéric Maillez, was driving past shortly afterwards and tended to Diana, who was still showing vital signs, with his limited medical supplies until the ambulance arrived. Emergency crews used an electric chainsaw to remove the car roof to extract the four from the car cleanly.

After attempting to stabilize Diana, the ambulance took her to hospital. Along the way, she suffered cardiac arrest and the ambulance stopped while AED and CPR were administered.

Within half an hour, Britain's ambassador to France, Michael Jay, was notified of the accident. He alerted the Queen's private secretary, Robin Janvrin, who was with the royal family at Balmoral.

Prince Charles apparently told Stephen Lamport, his Private Secretary: "They're all going to blame me, aren't they? The world's going to go completely mad, isn't it? We're going to see a reaction we've never seen before. It could destroy everything. It could destroy the monarchy."

The ambulance arrived at Pitié-Salpétrière Hospital, at 2.01am, and Diana immediately underwent surgery. At 4am, the princess, who was 36 the previous month, was pronounced dead, though it was some time before the rest of the world was told.

"Diana's body arrived in a condition of serious haemorrhage and shock," anaesthesiologist Dr. Bruno Riou told the media gathered outside. "An urgent surgery showed a severe wound to the left pulmonary vein. Despite the closure of this wound and the two-hour external and internal cardiac massage, no official respiratory circulation could be established."

Then Operation Overlord swung into action – the official plan to repatriate the body of a royal who dies abroad, though anyone up with history will know this was the same name used for the D-Day landings in France in 1944.

Accompanied by Prince Charles and Diana's sisters, Lady Jane Fellowes and Lady Sarah McCorquodale, Diana's body left the Paris hospital at 6pm, bound for England aboard an aircraft of the Queen's Flight. About an hour later, it touched down at RAF Northolt, north-west of London, where a ceremonial guard carried her coffin, draped in the royal standard, to a waiting hearse and on to St James' Palace.

Diana had been prophetic in her belief, dating from when she and Charles were courting; she had said she knew she would never be Queen of England. She said she didn't know how she knew it, she "just felt it". Her candle had burned out, but her legend will endure, as Elton John sang at her funeral in the same Westminster Abbey where she had wed.

Back in Paris, just hours after the crash, Mohamed Fayed was in a morgue, looking down at a body labelled "No. 2146". He saw his 42-year-old son Dodi looking "like a little boy, at peace".

23 Hold the Entire Paper

L
ike any newsroom, the Mail on Sunday's had TVs everywhere, though the BBC were still three months from launching their rolling news service, News 24, and BBC World was the only live channel the broadcaster had. Presenter Kay Burley was called from her bed at 3.30am to front Sky's special coverage.

There was a swift recall of MoS staff, too, many of whom had not long got back home, some already tucked up for the night. Paris-based reporters and stringers, were scrambled, too, to get on the biggest story since the paper launched in 1982. Execs began returning, including editor Jonathan Holborow and his deputy Rod Gilchrist. Those who lived further afield reappeared at intervals throughout the night. Arrangements were made with the press hall to expect numerous new editions, at times to be decided, as events unfolded through Sunday morning.

The next papers scheduled to be out the door in Kensington were the Monday editions of the Daily Mail and early morning London Evening Standard. The MoS, it was decided, would plug the gap until then.

The paper had been completed and the first job was to strip out some pages further back in the issue, to enable us to move previously important stories out of the way for the Diana content. It meant redesigning pages and refitting words and pictures and sending them off to the printers.

I immediately offered to help and vividly recall getting a very bemused look from the executive editor, Phil Bullen, as if to say: "But you are the bloke who fixes the computers..."

He had clearly forgotten that I had trained him on the page editing system we were using – and had worked alongside him in production just a few years earlier. I put this down to the stress of the situation and shrugged it off, helping out anyway until more page subs arrived. Nobody quite made it in their pyjamas but this was definitely dress-down Sunday.

I forget how many editions we cranked out but the Diana coverage grew with each one as more became known and backgrounders were assembled.

We had a few pages ready for an obit supplement in case the Queen Mother died – she went in 2002 - and refreshed them periodically. But nothing for Diana as her death at just 36 was so premature and unexpected.

Our front page shortly before her demise had been confirmed, was headlined: "Diana very grave after car crash", with the strap-line "4am: Tragedy for Princess as Dodi is killed". It was updated within an hour or so. Perhaps the use of the word 'grave' was not in the best taste, with the benefit of hindsight.

There were calls made to royal press officers' home numbers, reflections were written on Diana's life; of her run-ins with the media, balanced with all her good work for charities, as well as witness statements from the scene, from police and hospital officials.

Her marital travails of course featured large, referencing the famous but now even more controversial Martin Bashir TV interview in which she said there had been "three people in the marriage, so it was a bit crowded" – a clear reference to Charles' enduring relationship with Camilla.

I covered a Charles event when I was on the Evening Mail in Slough. It was a charity gig, mid-afternoon at a stately pile somewhere near Ascot racecourse. We had come out of the hat on a "royal rota", that reduced the number of Press at routine events.

The amusing thing was seeing a line of hyphenated, middle-aged ladies preening as Charles began to leave, saying their farewells while pushing their taffeta-dressed daughters towards him as if they were part of some kind of posh totty buffet. This was before he had met Diana and was still presumably busy playing the field. I was standing in an area roped off for the media but beside Charles's Aston Martin sports car. There was a bottle of Champagne and bunch of flowers (and not the sort you'd get from the petrol station) on the passenger seat. I often wonder if Camilla was the intended beneficiary, though there had been many other 'runners and riders'.

The nation chose sides when Charles and Diana split in 1992 after more than a decade of marriage and the outpouring of grief that followed her death showed which camp they had pitched up in.

The movie The Queen, starring Helen Mirren in the title role and Michael Sheen as Tony Blair, dramatised but reflected the royals' remoteness that week, amplified by them being closeted in Scotland on their huge estate at Balmoral, and shone a light on the panic behind the scenes that followed the crash in Paris.

Protocol dictated so much – but there was no guiding precedent. After the Queen's initial reluctance, Diana's funeral was based on the one planned for the Queen Mother, codenamed Tay Bridge (the monarch's is London Bridge).

In the days leading up to the funeral on Saturday, September 6, there were calls for the Queen to address the nation on TV and come down to London

– and also to allow the royal standard to fly at half-mast over Buckingham Palace. She gave in to all the demands, but only after initially insisting that she would not, and that there was no precedent.

The Queen's failure to grasp what the public were feeling fuelled huge resentment and newspaper polls showed growing numbers turning against the idea of monarchy.

In the lead-up to the funeral, I made the short walk from the office to Kensington Palace, which had been Diana's home, a couple of times, to see a small knot of flowers grow into a giant carpet, complete with candles, teddies and poems, left by tearful mourners from many parts of the world.

The public's reaction and outpouring of grief was bemusing to many – even to some in my office – but it showed how Diana touched lives that could not be further removed from her own privileged circle, one in which she refused to be wholly cocooned and trapped.

We had seen revelations about her life and marriage down the years – and how Diana had learned to "play" the same Press that was being used against her. She used to meet surreptitiously with trusted Daily Mail reporter Richard Kay in his car, not far from the palace, spilling the odd little nugget to ratchet up the pressure on "The Firm", or just "Them" – her nicknames for the royals.

There were recordings from elsewhere that exposed the closeness of Charles's relationship with Camilla; Charles at one point embarrassingly wishing he was her tampon and that he wanted to "live inside her trousers".

Andrew Morton's biography, Diana: The True Story revealed details of her eating disorder, bulimia, brought on by the stress of being constantly in the public eye, and by the insecurity of her marriage.

She nevertheless managed all kinds of subterfuge to sneak out to visit homeless shelters and to meet others who had fallen through the State's flimsy safety net. She was president or patron of more than 100 charities and took a keen interest in each one. That work schedule would have been punishing enough, without the constant drama playing out around her at every turn.

There were recriminations all round after her death. The media fended off accusations of its complicity in it, pointing instead to those who bought the magazines and newspapers that were festooned with gossip and photos of her and fuelling demand for ever more intrusive material in a kind of self-fulfilling loop.

Although unable to fully defend herself, Diana and her advisors had been able to circle the wagons around William and Harry, as newspaper editors agreed to allow them to grow up without unfair intrusion, at least until they reached seniority.

Indeed, the one thing Diana did effectively was to shield her boys. Thus, with her gone, it was one of the more troubling aspects of her funeral to see William and Harry having to walk behind her coffin, with the whole world watching their every step and expression. Had it been Charles who had died, you can bet Diana would have fought to her last breath to make sure the boys had a private car to the church and not be put through such an evidently scarring ordeal.

Harry has said that walking behind his mother's coffin when he was only 12 was something no child "should be asked to do". He later told the BBC he doesn't "have an opinion whether that was right or wrong", but "looking back on it", he is now "glad to have been part of the day".

The prince also paid tribute to his father for the way he took care of them after Diana's death. "One of the hardest things for a parent to have to do is to tell your children that your other parent has died," Harry said. "How you deal with that I don't know, but he was there for us."

William, who was 15, recalled more recently: "It was a very long, lonely walk. I felt that if I looked at the floor and my hair came down over my face, no-one could see me."

The funeral is remembered for many things, in particular Sir Elton John singing a special version of Candle in the Wind, and for Diana's brother Charles, Viscount Althorp's cutting speech, which ripped into all and sundry, with rank no barrier to his barbs.

He started with the Royal Family – who stripped her of her royal title, saying, "Diana was someone with a natural nobility, who was classless... and had no need of a royal title." Then he turned his ire on the media, who he said "constantly sought to bring her down". He said he always knew the Press would "get her in the end", adding "but not even I could imagine that they would take such a direct hand in her death, as seems to be the case."

He pointed out the irony that "a girl given the name of the ancient goddess of hunting was, in the end, the most hunted person of the modern age".

His words were greeted with a ripple of applause that began in the royal parks, where many thousands watched on big screens, and grew to a crescendo. Then it spread from the back of Westminster Abbey to the front, as the royals sat in an awkward silence that was lost on nobody who witnessed it.

I had watched the funeral from home in Northamptonshire before driving down for my shift that Saturday. The M1 was littered with flowers that had been tossed at the hearse as it ventured north to her final resting place on an island in a lake at Althorp, just outside Northampton. Floral remnants were evident at intervals all the way down to Swiss Cottage.

Naturally our paper that weekend was given over largely to the funeral of a remarkable woman who touched the hearts of millions. Her death reined in some media excesses, for a while at least, though the phone-hacking scandal that led to the closure of the News of the World in 2011, the arrest and jailing of journalists, huge payouts to celebrities and a lasting cloud of suspicion over key figures at The Sun and Mirror, only reinforced Private Eye's labelling of our national press as the Street of Shame.

While working in West London near the beginning of my career, I played football for the London Evening News. Two team-mates, Greg Miskiw and Alex Marunchak, were to become embroiled in the News of the World phone hacking affair many years later. Alex was never charged but Greg got six months in stir.

I find it truly shaming that the second part of the Leveson Inquiry into press malpractice, which was halted until after prosecutions of News International staff, was binned by the Conservative Government in 2018. It ill serves the public and the media and leaves the clear conclusion that the Government had a face-saving agenda uppermost in its decision-making.

A tightening of media rules would have threatened the unhealthy revolving door between Fleet Street and Government. As we have two former Times columnists holding key levers of power, Boris Johnson and Michael Gove, the prospects of Leveson resurfacing are non-existent.

The tragedy of it all is that Diana, now in her tranquil island grave at Althorp, was never afforded any kind of peace while she was alive. Her marriage to Charles, which she had, by many accounts had grave misgivings about, should never have gone ahead.

The biggest losers were of course her children, William and Harry. Her death shaped them in different ways and to different extents.

But I also wonder how Diana's relationship with the media – she died, of course, before the social media age – would have changed had she lived. She already had a global reach – and even today, in death, manages to fill acres of newsprint. But Queen of the internet? That would have been a certainty.

She soon cottoned on about how to manipulate the mainstream media. Imagine what she could have done with a Twitter account...

24 *King Kenny's Bouncy Balls*

O ne of the great things I have found down the years is that, even if a job was feeling stale or routine, there was often a freelance project that I could take on to get me fired up. One of the best was in 1998. And it proved a bizarrely exciting experience.

Paul Fairclough guided Stevenage Borough into the FA Cup fourth round, uncharted territory for the club. They were rewarded with a home tie against

Newcastle United. It was to be a monster.

Newcastle, with the likes of Alan Shearer, Faustino Asprilla, John Barnes, David Batty and David Ginola on the payroll, had finished second in the Premier League in the previous season, managed by former, Celtic, Liverpool and Scotland star Kenny Dalglish.

Stevenage had finished third in the non-League Conference with a side assembled at a cost of about £16,000. Come matchday, Stevenage were limping along, 15th in the table.

Within a couple of days of being drawn together, the clubs were entangled in a dispute over the match venue. Boro had been forced to move their previous season's third-round home tie against Birmingham City away from their 6,000-capacity Broadhall Way stadium and played it at St Andrews, City's home ground.

Newcastle initially demanded the same treatment but the Football Association were not having any of it. They had been unhappy at the previous Boro venue switch - which brought the smaller a club a bigger payday - and backed Stevenage in hosting the tie at Broadhall Way, which would be expanded from a 6,000-capacity venue to more than 8,000 thanks at a temporary stand erected at the visiting supporters' end.

But the furore, once began, had a life of its own and was even discussed on BBC TV's Newsnight. Take-no-prisoners host Jeremy Paxman at one point asked Newcastle manager Kenny Dalglish if his reluctance to head south made him "a big girl's blouse".

Paul Fairclough recalls: "Once the draw had been made, I had a phone call from Kenny – but I didn't know it was him at first. I could barely understand his accent and thought it was one of the lads taking the mickey.

"This Scottish-voiced person on the other end was going on about how he was worried about different things but I didn't take too much notice. Shortly afterwards, their safety guys turned up at our ground. But our chairman, Victor Green, who never missed an opportunity, seized on a chance to escalate the publicity. By the time they got down here, the television cameras were waiting for them."

Whether or not Victor had vowed to "milk this for all it is worth", as claimed by Newcastle's Freddy Shepherd, the die was cast – the game gripped the public's attention. The Sun dived in as match sponsors, and Sky chose to broadcast it live on Sunday, January 25.

Amid the growing rancour, which the media focus undoubtedly helped to fan, Stevenage still had a match to prepare for - for many of the players, the game of their lives. Inevitably they would have fears.

Cloughie's approach was informed by a strong understanding and deft use of psychology. On England C duty, his players are encouraged to stand in front of the squad and voice their greatest fears. It was a tactic he first deployed to great effect before Stevenage's tie with Newcastle.

"Everybody just opened up with the sports psychologist guy Paul brought in," recalls striker Giuliano Grazioli. "I wasn't sure they would. But they spoke openly of their fears: about playing in front of the Sky cameras for the first time, live, with the world watching. Being embarrassed. Losing 10-0 and all your family there seeing you get ridiculed.

"Paul went through those worries one by one, alleviating all that fear. One of the big ones was fitness, so he brought in a three-week programme to build stamina and endurance.

"He had crowd noise at training – long before it was used for matches in lockdown – and had one half of the players decked out in Newcastle shirts in training set-ups, just to get us used how the game might look. Small things, but they all added up.

"Come the day, we weren't worried about anything. We went a goal down after three minutes, yet we ended up getting a replay. And we could or should have won it."

Cloughie recalls: "The tie had everything, including the bullying element to it. Our chairman was very good at manipulating the press and Newcastle responded in completely the wrong way when the draw was made.

"Newcastle were portrayed as the big, bad bullies trying to quash the little ant and it captivated the world. We had film crews from all over – and Sunderland and Middlesbrough fans were buying our shirts to wind up their Newcastle-supporting pals."

That Stevenage's rag-tag group of players – most

of whom worked day jobs, from metalworker, to delivery driver and painter-decorator – faced their biggest fears and won at least a moral victory is testament to brilliant preparation.

I acted as an ad hoc media officer in the run-up to the game, speaking to pals I knew on the nationals and giving them some insight into the more interesting players in the squad.

The Sun ran special Boro wrap-rounds with their paper each day the week of the match. They ran down every angle they could think off... such as stunting up a picture of decorator Robin Trott with a Page 3 girl who was wearing pretty much only body paint in Boro's distinctive red and white diagonal stripes. The build-up was frenetic. It was fun. There seemed to be a new controversy every day. You just hoped the game could live up to the hype.

The programme was a joy to work on and I used pretty much all my production skills – starting with the design concept for a 64-page, full-colour one-off, priced at £2. I commissioned words, and also wrote stuff, including interviewing Jimmy Greaves, who was a Sun columnist; Sky commentator Andy Gray and Newcastle's England winger John Barnes, as well as handling all the production. I even had to design some of the ads.

I managed to track down John Fahy, who scored for Bedford Town in a 1964 FA Cup win against Newcastle – with the added twist that he was living in Newcastle –New South Wales.

A Mail on Sunday colleague, Bob Cass, interviewed

Kenny Dalglish, which was just as well as Newcastle were generally a nightmare to deal with. I had found much more co-operative clubs lower down the game's pecking order even than Boro.

Newcastle were on a hiding to nothing and didn't fancy the trip south at all. Defender Steve Howey recalls: "It was their five minutes of fame and they were in the papers all the time, from the time of the draw until we played, giving it 'the big 'un'.

"I can't repeat the words said before we travelled but you can imagine we were thinking, 'We'll go down there and show these' and basically just go to town on them."

What was remarkable about Stevenage's run to the fourth round was that they so easily could have gone out of the competition at Carshalton Athletic in the first round. They clung on stubbornly for a 0-0 draw in Surrey and won the replay 5-0. Boro needed another replay in the next round to see off Cambridge United and were then drawn at Championship side Swindon Town.

Grazioli got the winner in horizontal rain and with a gale-force wind driving straight down the ground after the Swindon goalkeeper tried to kick the ball clear and it arced back in front of his own unprepared defenders, who were robbed and Jason Soloman set up Grazioli's sliding finish.

Come the big day, I got to Broadhall Way early to savour the build-up – only to find the press box oversubscribed and I had no seat. Victor Green made sure I got to watch the game from the director's lounge instead. So I had a great view of the game; I was warm, there were cups of tea on tap, with biscuits – plus the bonus of live commentary and instant replays on the TV behind me. I was like a pig in muck.

It was a jolt to see Shearer, back after a knee injury, wheel away after scoring just three minutes into the game but thereafter Stevenage had by far the best of it, with Newcastle's Shaka Hislop the busier of the goalkeepers.

Cloughie says: "I had two parrots on my shoulder all week: one saying we'd get slaughtered and the other that we might win.

"The early goal was a massive blow and Shearer gave me a look as he ran past me with his arm aloft. But I looked at our players and knew they had been prepared for this. Really prepared."

When Grazioli headed in Gary Crawshaw's in-swinging corner just before half time, it felt that the game would never restart. There was bedlam as the Stevenage players were submerged by ecstatic Boro fans in front of the East Stand. In truth, Boro were largely untroubled in seeing out the game.

Striker Neil Trebble, a former soldier whose saved header brought about the corner for Boro's goal, was disappointed not to have won the game, saying: "We had a goal disallowed for offside and we had the chances to win it." Indeed, Neil's wickedly curling free-kick almost forced an own goal from Rob Lee.

Then came the seemingly faux handshakes, excuses and wind-ups. Fairclough recalls: "I don't think Kenny rebuffed me after the match but, put it this way, he went inside very quickly and I never saw him again until the replay."

Victor Green was not slow to weigh in, adding that centre-back Mark Smith had £15m England striker Shearer "in his back pocket" – which went down like a lead balloon on Tyneside.

Dalglish blamed the hard pitch, the swirling wind – and the even ball, which was "too bouncy". The problem with that is the ball they played with was endorsed by... Kenny Dalglish.

Grazioli recalls the evening's celebrations: "It was a Sunday so there weren't too many places open for us to go, but we found this club in south London and headed there.

"On the way, we got a call from someone at Stevenage telling us we had to be up at 5am next morning because we were appearing on The Big Breakfast on TV, which killed our fun a bit. We still went out and made it to the studios for the show. We were interviewed by Denise van Outen, which wasn't a bad way to spend a Monday morning. I remember walking down my road later that day and seeing scores of people surrounding my house. At least 50 were journalists. My grandad was on my step, shouting, 'What shall I do? What shall I do?' It was mayhem.

"I could not play in the replay because I had picked up an injury at Gateshead the week before. It would have been great to have appeared at St James' Park. It felt like an opportunity lost."

In Graz's place stepped Paul Thompson – a proper

Geordie, who had been injured for the first match and had signed for Boro from Gateshead. "One of the things that cheered me while I was out injured," said Tommo, "was a note from Alan Shearer. He saw something about me in the paper up there and wrote to me.

"He'd had the near-same injury and it gave me a big lift. I never imagined I'd be playing against him."

And so to the replay at St James' Park, with a home tie in the last 16 of the FA Cup against Tranmere Rovers, who knocked out Sunderland, awaiting the winners. The irony was not lost on some people that Newcastle, having wanted the tie played at their stadium, at least got their way at the second time of asking.

There was clearly plenty of niggle left over. Fairclough remembers how one of the Newcastle players thumped him in his back as he was walking on the pitch before the game.

But the most bizarre occurrence was the receipt of a fax that cost former Tottenham captain and Stevenage defender Graham Roberts his job as manager of Yeovil Town. Smarting from seeing Stevenage hold up his transfer from Boro to Yeovil, Roberts was allegedly involved in sending a controversial fax to St James' Park on the afternoon of the replay.

The fax was apparently on Yeovil Town headed paper and contained disparaging comments about Stevenage. It apparently read: "We are not all arse-holes in the Vauxhall Conference."

When news of the fax was made public, Yeovil

binned Roberts. It is still a mystery how the fax found its way into the Boro dressing room, to be discovered by club's kit man. But it had to have been put there by someone in the Newcastle camp who knew it would be found.

In his programme notes, Dalglish denied he had sought to take credit from Stevenage for the first match. "I said it was the biggest day in their history and everything had gone brilliantly for them. And I would not pretend a Premier League club drawing at a Conference side is a great result.

"Stevenage will be treated with the respect they deserve." That, in context, felt like a barbed comment.

The opening goal that cold but dry Wednesday night on Tyneside was one that still gets a rise out of Stevenage fans, of whom there were plenty in the 36,705 crowd or watching on TV. Today's goal-line technology would have backed up their case that it should not have been allowed – but it is, of course, a recent innovation.

After 16 minutes, Shearer headed a far-post cross back across goal and Mark Smith appeared to have scooped it clear with a stunning overhead kick–even the home crowd were semi-muted in their initial response. But referee Peter Jones awarded the goal and Shearer quickly celebrated to make sure the official didn't have time for any second thoughts.

"Even now, I'm sure it didn't go in," Smith swears. "I don't know how that goal could have been given. It was nowhere near over the line."

A computer reconstruction by Sky later showed the ball didn't fully cross the line - so the goal should not have stood. And in January 2021, when Tottenham played lowly Marine in the FA Cup, Shearer, a match pundit was shown a mock-up of Smith clearing the ball. Gary Lineker teased him, saying he had got away with one.

Shearer smiled and said: "I wasn't certain it had cleared the line but I just made sure I started celebrating quickly as it was unlikely the ref would rule it out."

There was a suspicion of offside about Newcastle's second goal, too, when Jon-Dahl Tomasson crossed for Shearer to score with a stooping header at the far post.

It was to Boro's immense credit that they fought back, with Gary Crawshaw hooking the ball in at Hislop's near post with 15 minutes to go. Paul Fairclough said that when Gary scored, he looked across at Newcastle's bench and saw fear.

Certainly United coach Terry McDermott had a face like thunder – there are pictures of him at the time. And the tackles suddenly had a bit of added spice. But it finished 2-1 to Newcastle all the same and the adventure was done.

However, in keeping with the general tone of the whole tie, Dalglish, when told of Cloughie's comments about the fear in the home camp after Boro's goal, said: "Well, he won't be looking across any more. He'll be back in the Vauxhall Conference".

Jaws dropped in the press room - and Paul was not impressed, saying later: "I haven't heard that myself but if he has said that then he's a very, very sad man.

"He shook my hand at the end but as a non-League manager I just wanted someone as big as Kenny Dalglish to say 'well done.' But he didn't. I'm disillusioned with that, although he's obviously got his reasons.

"They are a big club and they could so easily go on now. Beating Stevenage Borough could turn their season and I hope they go on and win it." In fact, Newcastle did reach the final, but lost 2-0 to Arsenal.

There was at least one happy postscript: A few days later, Mark Smith received Shearer's shirt in the post. It seems they are not all arseholes in the Premier League.

In 2011, history struck again when the clubs were drawn together in the FA Cup Third Round at Stevenage's Lamex Stadium.

The former principal protagonists had long since left the stage and there were no old scores as such to settle. The fans, of course, would disagree. But Boro, by then a League club, deservedly won 3-1 – no dodgy goals that didn't go over the line and no rancour off the field.

And how those Boro fans celebrated. As did Mark Smith. They say if you wait long enough...

25 Kia Ora in Kiwiland

New Zealand is a world away – 11,386 miles to be pedantic – but more than far enough to provide a decent perspective on life back in Britain. The standing joke is that when you land in Auckland, you need to put your watch back 30 years. Further, if judged by one of the first cars I saw there: a Ford Consul, just like those my twin uncles, Jim and Keith, drove in the late 1960s.

You could argue, with more recent events, particularly the contrast in the way both countries handled the Covid-19 pandemic, that the gap has closed and may even have been reversed.

The Land of the Long White Cloud (Aotearoa in Māori) was my home for almost five years - and source of employment for six more after I returned to the UK. Living there is an experience I would recommend to anyone feeling increasingly Victor Meldrew about life in Brexit Britain. It was enriching in so many ways.

I had just lost a big freelance contract when I saw an advert in the journalists' trade mag, UK Press Gazette, for sub-editors on the daily New Zealand Herald in Auckland. After some digging, I worked out that I would just squeak through the points-based immigration system by hitting the bar of 100. It took into account education and experience. Plus the job had to have been advertised unsuccessfully in New Zealand.

So I applied, had an interview in London, agreed a deal and was given a contact on the news desk to ring for some general advice on moving and life there. George Butler had an English wife, Karen, had lived in the UK and had worked for the Daily Express. He was able to give me a decent steer on what my family and I could expect from our new life down under.

I'd never visited New Zealand, and a trip to Australia with my mum in 1985 scarcely counted. But the time felt right for a new challenge. Not long after that trip to Aussie, I had looked at working there and found there were reciprocal agreements between the countries. But they seemed one-sided: To go out there, Brits had to have a decent amount

of collateral behind them, as well as being on a re-
quired-jobs list, but there were plenty of low-paid
jobs near Earls Court for Aussies.

New Zealand would accept me, and, after three
years, I could get a Kiwi passport that would give
me free entry to Australia if I wanted to move there,
side-stepping the direct route. (That back door was
increased to five years while we were living in NZ).

We took off from a cold and very wet Heathrow
not long before midnight on New Year's Eve, 2004,
and saw in the New Year somewhere on the way to
France. After a stopover in Hong Kong, we arrived in
Auckland mid-afternoon on January 2, a bank holiday, to brilliant sunshine and blue sky.

The Herald gave me two weeks to settle in and
put us up in an ultra-modern apartment on Princes
Wharf, on the waterfront, bang in the heart of the
city. Moored just down the quay was the Soren Lar-
sen - tall-ship star of UK TV show The Onedin Line,
which had been immensely popular in New Zealand, too.

Next morning, as I drew the blinds, dressed not
entirely fully, all I could see out of one window was
the giant letter "O". On closer inspection, it was the
290-metre-long cruise liner Oosterdam, which had
moored early doors with great stealth. It was as if
someone had sneaked an office block in overnight.
Almost 2,000 passengers were being disgorged and
the fleet of cabs waiting for them went all the way
round the wharf.

The visitors were likely heading beyond Auckland

to Rotorua or the Coromandel Peninsula or perhaps even to catch the ferry for Waiheke Island and its vineyards.

After looking at different potential areas to live, we settled on Orewa, 30 minutes' drive north, over the Harbour Bridge, on the Hibiscus Coast. The bridge is a wonder in itself. Built as a four-lane crossing, it now has eight - with two each way having been added courtesy of Japanese engineering. Locals dub it the 'Nippon Clip-on'. Each weekday, to prepare for the morning and evening rush hours, giant lifting vehicles transfer the concrete-block separation barrier across by one lane to ease peak traffic flow.

Below is the Waitematā Harbour, home to the Southern Hemisphere's largest collection of yachts and marinas. When I lived in Auckland, planners were debating using an old oil tank wharf as the site of a new super stadium fit for the All Blacks and big music events, though that didn't happen. Viaduct Harbour did, though – a vibrant mix of hotels, restaurants and bars - but not until after we left in mid-2009.

The City of Sails is overlooked by the Sky Tower, one block across from the Herald's old offices in Albert Street; it is 328m high, and you can see up to 80km (50 miles) from the top decks. For more fearless visitors, there is a chance to bungee off a platform just below the observation level. I didn't fall for that one.

I found the pace of life very agreeable. For at least

three years, the headaches that had plagued me back in Blighty never recurred. Winters were mild in the sub-tropical climate and I can barely recall a frost.

I missed the seasons. The most memorable major shift came with a temperature dip in May and near-biblical rains around November. You'd get the proverbial 30 days and 30 nights, and the rain would clout our steel roof so hard that the TV satellite signal broke up with 'rain fade'. Like Ireland, New Zealand is a verdant country for a reason.

One of the first things I noticed was how many more older men there seemed to be. I think that goes with the lower levels of stress. Our neighbour, Jack, was in his 90s and had served in the NZ forces as part of the clean-up in Japan after Hiroshima. He had to have all manner of small growths removed over the years, but he got about well enough. He had been a nurseryman for years and still grew veggies in his yard and would leave bunches of runner beans or whatever crop he had going at the time on our doorstep without even a note.

He'd never take any money, even though he could have done with it: it broke my heart one winter day to see him and his wife, Ivy, in bed in their thick coats to fend off the cold.

We had decent neighbours. One couple, Kel and Margaret, whose house was at the top of our shared drive, loved dogs but did not want to commit to owning one. Instead, they often took ours, two Brussels Griffons, Lizzie and Murphy, for a walk. One day, Lizzie sneaked out under our metal gate and found her way next door. Margaret was having a nap and woke to find her at the bottom of her bed, sleeping.

In front of us was a family we didn't get to know. But he had a job as an entertainer. He was an Austin Powers tribute act and had a VW all done out in psychedelic colours. He was also good for trampolines and bouncy castles. I felt like telling him to beee-have.

There is a heavy oriental influence in the population, which reflects New Zealand's location within the Asia-Pacific region, as well as a large number of Pacific Islanders. The giant Samoans who moved our furniture were awe-inspiring to watch, one guy lifting a wooden-framed three-seater leather sofa over the balcony down to the roof of the removals truck, where his pal was standing to collect it. Stairs? Why bother with them?

Ah, removals. There is a thing among expat Brits in NZ who struggle to settle, often with the pull of family a long way back home. We knew three families who had yo-yo'd between NZ and the UK, unable to work out quite where they wanted to be. Sometimes their shipping container would only just have arrived in Tauranga, in the Bay of Plenty, after a six-week journey, but they had already decamped back to Britain.

I recall walking into the Herald newsroom for the first time, thinking I'd found the library by mistake as it was so quiet. My colleagues probably had to make bigger adjustments to me than the reverse - working out my sense of humour and occasional use of Cockney rhyming slang.

I used it as a measure of friendly cultural 'revenge' for being inflicted with some odd NZ words and phrases, such as "ute" - for sports utility vehicle - and the use of "farewelled", as in saying goodbye to someone who had died. Olympic athletes didn't finish first, second or third, winning gold, silver or bronze, they "medalled".

Then, of course, there were the vowel shifts. I recall being asked one day if I had a pin. A safety pin? I asked. No, they had meant a pen. And don't get me started on the fush and chups (kahawai and hoki are very good, by the way and I have seen hoki in UK supermarkets).

I learned of the resourceful Kiwi "No.8 wire" mentality – ingenuity at using some scrap to solve a technical problem – and picked up on skills that I had never imagined. We had an office fishing trip on the Hauraki Gulf one day and I marvelled as sports editor Chris Allen balanced himself at the front of the speeding boat and chatted nonchalantly as it pitched and twisted in the swell, while he coolly gutted a fish with a very long and very sharp knife. I could only wince and have the air ambulance ready on speed dial.

There were South Africans, Fijians, Aussies, Brits and of course Kiwis in a very cosmopolitan office. One morning, we had a visit from 007. Sean Connery was on the board of Independent News and Media, the paper's owners, and was there for a meeting. (They probably used to say meetings were about ten-nish just to see if he brought his racket with him). We were stirred but not overly shaken.

Weekends, if we were not working Sunday, were all about jaunts to beaches, such as the famed black sand one at Piha, with its imposing lion-shaped rock and rolling breakers so beloved of surfers. Getting there involved a wonderful scenic drive through the natural rainforest of the Waitākere Ranges, where you can stop off to see the delight-fully-named Fairy Falls.

To the north, we'd go to the quaint market town of Warkworth or, closer to home, to the Whangaparāoa Peninsula, with its beaches either side of its narrow tip and yet where you can feel like Man Friday – with barely a footprint in sight at times, and watch peacocks roam free in Shakespear Regional Park.

Closer to Auckland, a short ferry ride across the harbour from the central business district, is the re-laxed bayside village of Devonport, with its host of great pubs and cafes, underground military tunnels and a Royal NZ Navy base. I always enjoyed going there for a meal – and, indeed, the ferry ride for great views of the city.

One of my favourite Auckland places was Mount Eden, now officially known as Maungawhau/Mount Eden following a 2014 Treaty of Waitangi claim settlement with 13 local (Māori) tribes. It is a dor-mant volcano cone, 196m high, and when we lived in NZ, you could drive all the way to the summit for stunning 360-degree views.

The crater, grassed now, is still well defined. It is named Te Ipu-a-Mataaho ("the bowl of Mataaho"), after a deity who is said to have resided there as "guardian of the secrets hidden in the Earth".

The capital, Wellington, is an eight-hour drive at best. To get copies of the Herald there, a truck would go halfway and meet one that had come up from the capital and offload. We went there only once, staying for a few days in a beautiful beachside house in Paraparaumu, just up the west coast.

We did the touristy thing and took the cable car: a stunning five-minute climb, to take in the famed panorama. If there was sport on at the "Cake Tin", as the Westpac Arena was nicknamed, you could almost save yourself the ticket money and watch from up there.

I could have happily spent more than just a couple of hours in the six-floor Te Papa Tongarewa museum, which showcases New Zealand history, culture and art. There is a huge waka – war canoe – when you arrive, and an "earthquake house".

Strap yourself in and experience what a major jolt can feel like, without the need to change your trousers. There were a few shakes while we lived in NZ but none that we actually felt.

We had one about 60 miles off shore once and I delighted I sending the news home, with a photo of a garden chair I had flipped over.

Being on the "Ring of Fire" has greater significance

for those living down country in Hawke's Bay, or in Tauranga, - where White island (Whakaari), 30 miles off the coast, erupted in 2019, killing 21 people.

And, of course, in Christchurch, the most English of Kiwi cities, which suffered a devastating 6.3-magnitude shake in 2011, with 185 killed in one of the country's worst natural disasters. It destroyed the cathedral's landmark spire and tower and led to many people resettling away from the city.

One of the first things that struck me about the people in NZ was their friendliness. We had been used to stand-offish Brits. As we walked through a park one morning, some teenage schoolkids were heading towards us. I was expecting a Kevin and Perry-type grunty response but got a very polite and clear "Gidday, how are ya?"

Soon after our arrival, we were joined by some high-profile visitors from our home shores: the British and Irish Lions rugby team. Their tour created huge excitement - plus a great deal of controversy, enough to keep both ends of our newspaper busy.

The 2005 Lions were managed by former England and Lions forward Bill Beaumont and coached by Sir Clive Woodward, who led England to World Cup glory in Australia in 2003. Some 20 of the 44-man team were English. The Kiwis viewed this as an unofficial World Cup because they were still smarting from finishing only third across the Ditch, as they call the Tasman Sea between NZ and Australia. National pride was at stake and the verbal jousting was fierce.

Local media took aim at the Lions' bloated back-room team, which included Tony Blair's spin doctor, Alastair Campbell, in charge of media relations, ahead of the three-Test series. Campbell was a reverse Midas, if truth be told. And all the over-elaborate preparation by the Brits backfired.

The All Blacks are known for going in hard and early – which was also NZ's strategy with tackling the 2020 coronavirus pandemic - and it took just two minutes of the First Test to define the series' path.

The Lions lost skipper Brian O'Driscoll with a shoulder injury after a suspected outlawed 'spear tackle' by the dreadlocked Tana Umaga and hooker Keven Mealamu, with the Irishman being lifted and thrown headfirst into the turf.

Four months later, the game's governing body, the International Rugby Board, condemned the two All Blacks' conduct. But the damage was done. It knocked the stuffing out of the Lions; there is nothing like getting your retaliation in first.

Off the paddock, the All Blacks were nice guys... One day in central Auckland, while walking to the office, I saw the squad ambling from their hotel to a gym nearby. There was no visible security (I guess they were clearly equipped to take care of themselves). Some kids approached them to sign autographs and have a chat and they stopped to do so.

You could not imagine that being the case with a Premier League team back in England, where they would be cosseted from view.

The All Blacks were a formidable force and won the series 3-0, with Daniel Carter, Richie McCaw and Umaga out-posterboying even Jonny Wilkinson. Rugby is what passes for religion in New Zealand. But it is not a broad church. Statistically, Kiwi households are not pleasant places for some women when the All Blacks lose. Thankfully, that is rare.

I used to marvel at people in the newsroom when an ABs game was on. They would all gather round the TV to see what haka the team would perform and then pay almost scant attention to the game itself. Some, either engrossed in work or not that interested, would casually ask, when you got back to your desk, "Which one did they do?"

The haka, an intimidating-looking ceremonial kind of dance, has been performed by All Blacks teams before internationals since 1905. But it has taken on a life of its own. If you look at film on YouTube of ABs tours of Britain in the 70s, they were much less impassioned, more like the hokey cokey - nothing like the clearly choreographed theatrics we get today and which stir the crowd into a pre-kick-off frenzy.

They have different versions, such as Ka Mate, commonly misinterpreted as a type of war dance. It is a challenge and "a celebration of the triumph of life over death". The Kapa o Pango dates from 2005 and is reserved for "special occasions". The prime distinction is that this one ends with the drawing of the thumb across the throat. Both feature lots of bulging veins and eyes and hearty thigh slapping.

Opposing teams are supposed to stand respectfully to answer the challenge. So you can imagine the response when John Eales got his Australian team-mates to turn their backs on the haka in 1996.

In the 2019 World Cup semi-final, England formed up in a 'V' shape, in response, which many Kiwis took to mean 'Victory'. Six of the England side also strayed across the half-way line, which is not meant to happen. Haka experts actually praised England's response, though, saying any side that met the challenge deserved respect - but England were still fined by the rugby authorities.

The only time I got to see the All Blacks in the flesh was at North Harbour Stadium, not far from Orewa, when they ran out winners by a merciless 91-0 against Fiji. Up the road from us in Silverdale lived Wayne 'Buck' Shelford. He ran a bar and is the hands-down winner when it comes to the toughest player ever to pull on an All Blacks jumper.

In a match against France, he was kicked in the nether regions, the studs ripping free one of his testicles from his scrotum. Incredibly, he had it stitched on the sidelines and played on until he was concussed in the second half. Oh, and he lost four teeth, too. I don't believe he ever had any trouble in his bar.

They love their sport in New Zealand. One Herald colleague used to joke that, rugby apart, it was the 'sitting down ones' they excelled at most - rowing, cycling, canoeing. And after one unimpressive display by the football team, the All Whites, I added, "Football, too!".

That wasn't always the case, though. New Zealand qualified for the 2010 World Cup in South Africa - and acquitted themselves very well. I was working back in the UK by then, producing world news pages for six regional NZ dailies and doing occasional sports features. In the run-up to the finals, I tracked down their captain, Ryan Nelsen, who was then at Blackburn Rovers.

He spoke of how, despite all the pressure of mates when he was younger, rugby was not the game for him. Nelsen, who later joined Tottenham, had played college football in the United States and said he was honoured to be leading the side to their first World Cup in 28 years and hoped they could hold their heads high when it was over.

They were drawn against Slovakia, Paraguay and Marcello Lippi's Italy and were widely expected to be the group's easy meat. But they were tougher to chew than expected. Near the end of their opener, it seemed they were about to lose to Slovakia and I was holding back a couple of papers so I could get the result and a celebration picture on their front pages.

As the clock ticked to 90 minutes, I typed out the first few pars, saying it was disappointment again and a likely early exit, with Italy up next. We were ready to send the pages when, after three minutes of stoppage time and with virtually the last kick, Winston Reid equalised.

Cue a hasty rewrite and an anxious wait for the pictures of the goal by an unheralded right back of Maori descent who had been living and playing his League football in Denmark. It earned him a big-money transfer to West Ham that summer.

The Kiwis were in dreamland after just seven minutes of their next match. Striker Shane Smeltz (once of lower-league Mansfield Town and AFC Wimbledon) astonishingly put the All Whites 1-0 up against Italy. The Italians equalised after 27 minutes yet they never looked like going on to win as Nelsen and Co held firm.

A win in Polokwane in their last group match would have taken New Zealand, implausibly, into the knockout phase, but they drew 0-0 with Paraguay. It at least meant they finished unbeaten - a point ahead of bottom-placed Italy. Ryan Nelsen had got his wish.

Those results did a little to boost football's popularity back home, but nothing to dent the supremacy of rugby union, rugby league and cricket; or as the Herald sports desk would have it, rugby union, rugby union and rugby union.

My local paper in Orewa amused me with its sports coverage, which featured log-rolling and woodchopping. For Brit expats craving a bit of Match of the Day, primetime TV sports action on a Saturday night featured netball. Mind you, the old Hitchin Gazette used to carry pigeon-racing results when I started there...

After I had been with the Herald for barely 18

months, we were hit with a bombshell. Our sub-editing operation was to be outsourced to an Australian company, Pagemasters, with just a handful of subs to be retained to do the section front pages.

I don't think any of us had seen it coming. There I was, 11,000-plus miles from the UK with potentially no job - or one with the outsourced firm, almost certainly on less money.

I got wind of the fact that Ant Phillips, of the Herald on Sunday, had been drafted in to run the new operation. I had worked a few shifts with him there and he gave me the new boss's name. I thought that if I was going to leave the Herald, I would at least try to climb the food chain. I later learned that the Herald had wanted me to stay. Bruce Davidson, who ran Pagemasters in Melbourne, called while I was on a shift at the Herald and I had to try to carry on a discreet job interview with my colleagues around me, wondering what was going on.

My range of experience in the UK apparently won the day and I joined as production editor - No.2 in the new firm.

Together with Sharleen Heijstra, our office manager, Ant and I inspected our new offices above the Herald's print plant in suburban Ellerslie and set about organising the kit and hiring 50 staff - including some understandably grumpy folk from the Herald. We were, after all, trying to sell a project that would see them taking a pay cut.

The media is a small pool in New Zealand, with few employment offerings - fewer now. Eventually we got the place up and running, including a number of staff straight out of university who were keen and bright and willing to learn.

It was a nice mix and I loved working there. It didn't stop me feeling empathy for those who didn't make the move and lost their jobs. There were some good, experienced people among them.

We were to be at the cutting edge. Whereas outside agencies similar to Pagemasters had supplied format pages – TV listings, horoscopes, racing fields and puzzles, this was the first time anywhere, so far as we could see, that an outsourced sub-editing operation had been set up to produce 'live' pages for a number of papers.

We had one team, mostly of ex-Herald staff, to tackle that paper's pages, and another to sort out the seven regional dailies we would be producing. The regionals culled a number of staff and we hired one or two from each centre, working from their homes, to ensure we had good local knowledge.

They were good times, some of the happiest I have known in the business. I think the people involved were a big part of that. There was some real young talent who were keen to learn and we had a good training and mentoring programme, with people largely willing to learn. I really felt I had made at least some small difference and a decent impression.

Later, we would do most of the Herald on Sunday, the weekly Aucklander series and some part-work magazines.

I was really proud of the operation, which was not without its speed bumps and upsets in the early days. We had any number of challenges each day, tinkering with workflow, gathering feedback from our clients and striving to improve.

Visiting regional offices and meeting a sea of unhappy faces who had been told we were in and some of them were out was not easy. But it was crucial to building relationships and I am heartened that even a good few years after I left, I am still in touch with a good number of those people, as well as more than a few ex-Pagemasters staff.

Bruce was around a lot during the early days and we had high-level meetings with APN types to negotiate, convincing them we could bring the papers on stream as planned.

I recall seeing a familiar face at one of these meetings. It is a small industry. Terry Quinn, who had been deputy editor at the Gazette in Hitchin when I was sports editor, was now living on the Gold Coast in Australia and a key player for Australian Provincial Newspapers. I was thrilled that he failed to recognise me.

He is one of the very few people I have ever failed to get on with. In Hitchin, he and the editor, Richard Wooldridge, had this policy of 'creative tension'... to cause the maximum annoyance to people to get them to produce their best work. I have never experienced it since, though there was a similar reign of terror at the Daily Mail under Paul Dacre where news conferences were famed for the level of expletives uttered and bollockings handed out. I have always thought that unnecessary.

Away from the office, we had a few bruising five-a-side encounters, including one when I was so determined to hold my own against him that I played with a pulled hamstring. I didn't remind him of our history at our meetings in Auckland - and think he is still none the wiser.

When I left NZ in mid-2009, I carried on working for Pagemasters from home in the UK, supplying daily world news pages: in effect our outsourced company was re-outsourcing work to me. I took the job on a trial basis as there were worries about the telecommunications but carried on until the work was taken back in house.

I was briefly transferred to help out on some north-east Aussie dailies, in Darwin, Cairns and Townsville, and then Rupert Murdoch took that work back in house, too.

I completed the set with Pagemasters by working for their London operation, which was a rather bizarre one. The Daily and Sunday Telegraph outsourced production and editing of a lot of their supplements to us and, after a time working in offices elsewhere in the city, we moved into the Telegraph's offices in Victoria - sometimes siting a desk away from our clients.

Pagemasters UK later went the way of the NZ operation, with work reclaimed by the titles. Its parent company, Australian Associated Press (AAP), was on its knees until a recent restructuring, albeit with a few hundred fewer staff. This was before the coronavirus crisis. The worry, as news outlets close, is that a shrinking media is being left in too few hands and unable to function as fully as it should. It reflects fewer shades of opinion, which is a bad thing.

Not long after we returned to the UK, my then-wife, Sarah, died of pancreatic cancer. It was a difficult time and worked helped to provide a welcome focus.

In 2014, I went back to visit New Zealand with my current wife, Pam. She loved the place. We did things and visited places that I had never got around to doing previously and we got engaged over lunch in a vineyard on Waiheke Island.

Auckland's War Memorial Museum is brilliant. And so is the new Viaduct Basin, where you can admire superyachts as you eat lunch or labour over a coffee in the sun.

We stayed with James Smith, a former Pagemasters colleague in the Bay of Plenty, walking with him up Mount Maunganui. We met up with another English former colleague, Paul Chapman, and his wife, Liz, nearby at their lovely home with sweeping views – and a donkey, Mr Bojangles, who I know would have been badly missed when he died.

Pam loved Sydney, where we spent five days enroute home. It had been her dad's dream to see the harbour and we walked down there every evening and just sat watching the people and the lights on the Harbour Bridge and the Opera House.

We went to Bondi, which was underwhelming and

thought Manly Beach so much better. The Zoo was stunning - you go in on a cablecar and work your way down past so many exotic animals - the koalas were almost hypnotic to watch, perched on tree-limbs in their eucalyptus-induced trances.

We had seen the cruise ship Oosterdam (yes, that one from 2005) in Auckland just before we left there. I was more decorously dressed this time. Then the bugger turned up in Sydney.

We watched from outside the Opera House as it reversed out of its berth beside Circular Quay, the lights on the bridge and Quay all ablaze as it caught the evening tide and we pledged to return one day.

Just like the Oosterdam.

26 Looking Back. And Ahead

D uring the mid-1990s, I went part-time at the Mail on Sunday and tried to build a publishing consultancy, in part to sell internet services to companies. I had meetings with the Wine Society, a big industry co-operative which had its headquarters in Stevenage, and North Herts District Council, based in Letchworth.

Neither was interested in having a presence online at that time. Perhaps that was merely testament to the fact I was not the sort of person to sell the Pope a double bed. Yet both organisations now see web services as being essential tools in their operation.

They would not dream of being without one. There were siren voices like my boss John Forbes and I at other newspaper groups, echoing the need for newspaper groups to venture into the brave new world. I believe that failure to grasp the nettle early cost the news industry and, it could be argued, also cost democracy dearly.

While newspapers were sitting back, Google was expanding rapidly from being just a search engine to become an entity that would steal newspapers' lifeblood – advertising - and turn itself into an unstoppable and, it seems, untaxable behemoth, with a power that frightens off governments from challenging it seriously.

Social media came along later, Facebook in particular, to have another bite at papers' content. The digital giants have been happy to work with the newspapers – broadcasting bits of their content but unwilling to share the rewards equably.

Thousands of news jobs have been lost, hundreds of titles have become unsustainable and closed, and some titles are online entities alone now - such as the Sporting Life.

There are 650 parliamentary constituencies but fewer than 300 have a daily newspaper in their area. Some have lost weeklies, too. That means a lack of local scrutiny.

Local newspapers have been hit particularly hard. They have put much of their content - by no means all of it – online and invested heavily in digital. But the results in terms of online advertising have not matched expectations.

They have been caught in a cleft stick, with two cost bases - print and digital, and only one serious revenue stream: print advertising. I know that 70 percent of my own group's income is from print ads, and I think that will be pretty typical.

Managements would love to ditch print – that much is clear from some of their decisions, such as big annual cover price increases and constant cuts in staff numbers and resources to feed shareholders' demands for annual returns.

But they can't because digital revenues, while inching up, based on clicks by readers online, are not plugging the income gap. That is as much about format, I believe, as anything. On a web page, it is too easy to scroll past ads or block them altogether. Readers hate intrusive pop-ups and click them away.

Ads on a printed page are in your face. You can't click them away. You can see why advertisers prefer them. But circulations are falling – though ripping away the staff who could provide something worth reading is not helping. From the inside, it feels like scorched earth management and it is dispiriting to see a much-needed industry hobbled.

I can't think of a parallel in any other industry, where newspaper owners give their content away online, then expect readers to pay for much of the same stuff in printed form the following day. This was a definite policy.

This has happened with grumbled compliance

from staff, while few readers have worked out what has been done. You can't kid them all, though.

You could argue that the demographics suggest younger people, if they read news at all, do so on their phone, while mostly older folk buy the newspaper. And there is much to that.

But if print content were more appealing to younger people, it would at least help.

The Mail group has tried to migrate people towards digital, offering free Kindles to those subscribing to the paper. It was a decent product, too. For about a year, I'd help get the first print pages on sport away before nipping down the corridor to help repackage stories for the Kindle, which mostly involved adding extra images (more than you could get in the actual paper) and rewriting headlines to fit.

And there is software that you can use on a computer to experience reading a paper on PC screen or tablet as you would on paper – with the added ability to search out words and phrases. We use that in a digital monthly magazine I write a column for, #Stevenage – one of a growing stable of titles.

Darren Isted, a former local paper editor who runs the outfit, produces digital football programmes, too – a media-rich offering where, instead of photos of the previous match, you get video, and the chairman or manager's notes are also video. It has added value.

Newspaper websites do, too, but the pop-ups deter people from lingering.

In our newsroom, we can monitor which stories people are clicking on and how long they dwell on them. Twenty-five seconds is considered a "good" time... in reality scarcely long enough read more than a few sentences. You wonder if they give up at the first ad break.

We can monitor the times people are online, too, and post stories at that time of the day to catch their attention. Digital deadlines are frequent through the day – and of course we can go live with anything that is breaking.

But there is still a prevailing attitude among management that digital is king, and it is the only future.

One day not too long ago, working for a regional daily, a digital bigwig came round and was introduced to everyone except our print team. He was standing immediately behind me when I heard him speaking of his regret that print was mopping up advertising revenues and digital ads were lagging.

I bit my tongue and went out for a coffee. How very dare print continue to pay his wages while his chums ignore print entirely and engage in an unwinnable battle with the likes of Google and Facebook... Print will continue to wither as much because of that attitude as through falling sales.

Any print sub-editor will tell you that managements have firmly nailed their colours to the digital mast: they are intent on a policy of managed print decline, removing resources at every opportunity.

We now have no freelances, only columnists who

write for free, fewer photographers and no dedicated investigative reporters. A few years ago, we had an award-winning young reporter, who exposed historical sexual abuse at a children's home.

We no longer have the luxury of being able to take someone off the rota to do such work. Society will be the poorer for it. And, as you devalue the content, so people are merely encouraged to turn away from it.

So, for print, it really is a case of death by a thousand cuts.

I say all this as someone who sees value in digital and that it may indeed be the future. But I can also still see a need for print and believe they can coexist in some form. I don't moan as someone who could have his job taken away in the digital versus print argument, though that is obviously the case.

The Oscar-winning movie Spotlight, which starred Michael Keaton, Rachel McAdams and Mark Ruffalo tells the story of how an investigative team on the Boston Globe exposed widespread abuse of young children by Catholic clergy and offers a salutary lesson.

Strip the staff away and such terrible wrongs will never be reported, to the detriment of society.

Marty Baron, the Globe editor, later moved on to the Washington Post, insisting when he was hired that 25 more journalists be taken on. The paper subsequently won two Pulitzer Prizes and added a lot of subscribers, for both print and digital, under his leadership. A bit of investment can go a long way.

Newspapers still have an important role in society as a whole but seem in many cases to have forgotten that. The focus is solely shareholder-driven. There are some brilliant, campaigning newspapers such as the Yorkshire Post, but as resources are stripped away, it becomes ever more difficult, if not impossible to sustain such work.

News editors are required to send someone to a three-car shunt where nobody is injured rather than let them dig into nasty deeds that need illuminating – all in the name of online clicks, feeding a 'this has only just happened, tell me all now' approach. The rush to publish also carries risks of mistakes that more reflection and thorough checking can mitigate.

And there is this new culture, too, of reporting what is happening in the echo chamber of Twitter and Facebook, in reaction to a story, rather than on the facts of the story itself. It makes people jump to rash conclusions.

I do fear for the future of print. While I hear people say, "but people are reading their news online", that much is true, and mostly on their phones or tablets rather than computers.

But not every story goes online - mainly the stuff intended and pitched to garner clicks, which earn small amounts of revenue. And it means stories that would have much less prominence in print are the ones bosses clamour for.

The subs' joke in this brave new world is: "Quick, hold the front page... new coffee shop opening".

That is a slight, frivolous exaggeration but it sums up a prevailing mood.

The pursuit of the more mundane must surely be boring for reporters. It would have turned me off very early in my career. I know of one very good young reporter whose first job was to traipse round different McDonald's outlets in the city and compare and contrast the offerings of a national franchise that supposedly churns out stuff to the same recipe in all its outlets, day after day.

The treatment of news now flies in the face of a quote I used by author Dame Rebecca West in a college project on newspapers: "A community needs newspapers for the same reason a man needs eyes: it has to see where it is going." A media unable to shine a light on wrongdoing leaves us all in a darker place.

I don't believe it is any coincidence that as print has retrenched, particularly local media, society has become more shameless and officialdom less accountable.

As a trainee, I sat in court for days at a time and we'd carry small stories on even minor offences such as shoplifting. It was manna for the local curtain-twitchers and I am convinced the broader shame helped to deter repeat offences and perhaps even an escalation of offences by those individuals.

We were able to also offer more balance – reporting mitigation or defence. You can't do that in a paragraph in a stick of magistrates' court reports. There may be a human tale behind even the least obviously significant case.

Facebook feeds give all stories much the same weight and prominence; Twitter has a character limit - printed papers can guide readers with design, position and headline size.

National media has been changed hugely by the advent of rolling, 24-hour TV news and, indeed, the internet. Take football. We've all seen the match by the time the paper has come out, hence you no longer get the blow-by-blow game account and focus more on the personalities and the controversies arising from a match - not always for the better, and certainly inviting more intrusion. Today there can be more debate on a VAR decision than the other good and less controversial things in a match. It is almost as if VAR has been dreamed up to feel the media monster.

The daily newspapers have become purveyors of views and opinion rather than news, and for much the same reason: by the time we get our paper, the big events have been done to death on rolling radio and TV bulletins. Thus, they don't so much describe events as the reaction to them. It is almost embarrassing for me that, having been an internet evangelist, the internet is now the biggest threat to my own job in print. I always envisaged the two working hand in glove, with one feeding the other.

I used that model when I was programme editor for Stevenage Borough FC and set up the club's first website. Some stuff from the programmes went online later, while emails to the website were used to help fill the programme, bringing it closer to the supporters. Now the club doesn't have a printed programme but a digital one.

My time in tech at the MoS undoubtedly lengthened my career, making me self-sufficient and I have had, down the years, a wide range and number of publishing projects, from putting together books and magazines to corporate brochures and websites for small businesses.

Latterly, I have been working back in local newspapers – so I have gone full circle. There has been one constant: whenever I have moved, it is not so much the work I miss as the people.

I have been fortunate to work with some wonderful people even though we haven't always been able to share office space.

This book has enabled me to revisit so many experiences - but there have been more that I have left undocumented. It has been a tremendous journey.

And I may not have started out with ink in my veins but I will always be a newspaperman at heart.

Acknowledgements

There are too many people to thank, but I must start with John Sellers, who edited this book. And to Rod Pascoe, formerly of The New Zealand Herald, for taking care of the New Zealand section.

Others I must thank include Andy Straughn - a man with more of my cuttings than me; Peter Higgs, Patsy John, Kit Galer, Nick Chapman, Keith Berners, Paul Fairclough, Giuliano Grazioli, Bernadette Lyford, Paul (Hopper) Duffett and Mike Cattermole.

I must also thank Pam for her patience and support and of course, my mum, Jean Ross, without whom none of this would have been possible.

If I have forgotten anyone, please don't sue me.

Love and thanks to all.

About The Author

 Paul has been a journalist since leaving college at 19, taking up an apprenticeship with his local paper and embarking on a career that included 35 years in Fleet Street and five more in New Zealand. But he has produced books for others, and done all manner of print and digital work - from books and corporate publications, football programmes and magazines to websites. He currently works for Reachplc in the East Midlands.

He had nine years on the cutting edge of newspaper publishing, when the printers were being forced out of the industry, and has seen times of turbulent change in a trade which, if anything, have been accelerating in recent years.

Paul is a proud Stevenage lad, though he spent the first four years of his life in South London after being adopted as a baby. But he has also lived in Devon, Northamptonshire, central London and New Zealand.

He now lives in Leicester with wife Pam, a retired healthcare professional. And they have two grown-up daughters.

Printed in Great Britain
by Amazon